THE GROWTH OF THE GOSPELS

To THE PRIEST WHO
first TAUGHT ME TO
LOVE THE gospels —
WITH ETERNAL GRATITUDE!
by.
July 1989

THE GROWTH OF THE GOSPELS

Neil J. McEleney, C.S.P.

PAULIST PRESS
New York/Ramsey/Toronto

Library of Congress
Catalog Card Number: 79-90141

ISBN: 0-8091-2243-X

Published by Paulist Press
Editorial Office: 1865 Broadway, New York, N.Y. 10023
Business Office: 545 Island Road, Ramsey, N.J. 07446

Printed and bound in the
United States of America

Contents

To Mary and Joe, Peg and Harold
and their families
with grateful love
this work is affectionately dedicated.

A Word Before You Start

This book has limited aims. It is not an introduction to Bible study. It will not explain everything you ever wanted to know about the Gospels. It will try to help you understand why the Gospels came to be written and how they gradually took their present shape. It will try to give you a "feel" for the Gospels and prepare you for your prayerful reading of them.

All you will need before you as you read this book is a Bible. But you must use that Bible as you read here. There is no substitute in the learning process for your own verification of what you are told. Page through the Gospels, make your own comparisons between them, note how the evangelists build on their predecessors. Ask why one or other Gospel writer added some phrase or section to his source or omitted part of what he found there. This the only way you will gain insight into the mind of the sacred author and make his Gospel speak to you personally.

When you finish your task here, move on to the works listed in the bibliography. There you can expand your knowledge, correct false impressions (hopefully, none derived from this book), and gain deeper insight into the complexities of the simple Gospel message. But this book would have *you* do the work, with a little guidance, so open your Bible and let's have at it.

What Happened to the "Gospel Truth"?

First, let's clear some ground. "It's the Gospel truth!" How often have we heard that phrase? Not very often of late, but it used to mean that something was as certain as it could be, as certain as what was written in the Gospels. This was an older generation's approach to the Gospels. What was written there recorded with absolute veracity exactly what was said and what happened in the life of Jesus Christ. The Gospels were to be taken at face value as reporting every word, every incident exactly as it transpired.

Why? Because the Gospels were the word of God to man. Since God does not lie, the Gospels were true as written. They were, after all, the memoirs of two apostles, Matthew and John, and of two companions of apostles, Mark (who worked with Peter) and Luke (who traveled with Paul). These four men wrote biographies of Jesus Christ while firmly in the grip of the Holy Spirit's guiding hand. As the products of God almighty, these Gospels were something one could swear by—the Gospel truth.

Recent interpreters of the Gospels, however, have noted several things which make us understand the

1

"Gospel truth" in a richer, truer way. They make the following points.

(1) Overemphasis on the divine element in Gospel production does little justice to the human. God habitually works through human agents, and he works with them as they are. If these human agents are to be authors, they must do the work entailed in authorship and not simply be lifeless, inert, unthinking pens in the Lord's hand, faithfully reproducing only what comes from above. Like the rest of us, they have to work to achieve; accomplishment does not come easily. This is an important point—the Gospels are not only the work of God, they are the work of man.

(2) The Gospels give ample evidence of not being exact reproductions of what was said or what took place in Jesus' lifetime. They are not literary film clips suitable for some ancient evening news or taped messages from the ministry of Jesus. What makes this fact clear is the cumulative evidence gathered by detailed study of the Gospels themselves. Take a few minutes to run through the evidence I shall now present for (a) inconsistencies in chronology, (b) the doublet (the same passage or incident occurring twice in the same work), (c) conflicting details, (d) discrepancies in quotations, even in important questions, and you will see why modern scholarship finds a more complex design in the Gospels than did scholars, say, of the last century.

(a) For instance, in three Gospels, Matthew, Mark, and Luke, Jesus runs the sellers out of the Temple near the *end* of his earthly ministry (Mt 21:12-13; Mk 11:15-17; Lk 19:45-46). In John's Gospel, Jesus does this as he *begins* his public ministry (Jn 2:13-17). All four Gospels describe the one incident, despite some variations in their narratives, for in the social, political, and economic conditions of those times, it is not likely that Jesus'

2

action would have gone unresisted twice. He seems to have acted vigorously in the Temple while at the height of his prophetic popularity and therefore while he was still a figure to challenge with caution. This being so, the chronology of the first three Gospels is preferable here; Jesus drove the sellers from the Temple near the close of his earthly ministry. But in any case, since all the evangelists describe the same incident, they cannot all be reporting its exact moment in the life of Jesus.

Take another case, the miraculous catch of fish. Two such hauls are reported in the Gospels, but are they really the same event? Luke 5:1-11 associates one catch with the call and mission of Jesus' first disciples and places it at the beginning of Jesus' ministry. John 21 reports the same miraculous catch of fish, again in association with a mission, this time that of Peter, but John places it after Jesus' resurrection. Who has exact chronology here, Luke or John? Perhaps neither. At any rate, they do not both report the exact moment of the catch.

(b) Sometimes, one Gospel writer will tell the same incident twice. Mark has a good example of this in chapters 6—8 of his Gospel. First of all, note the parallel pattern in his Gospel's structure. (See the chart on the following page.)

The parallels between chapters 6—7 and chapter 8 of Mark are not absolutely perfect. After all, the elaborate account of Jesus walking on the water (Mk 6:45-52) is hardly equivalent to the mere mention of his getting into a boat and crossing over to an opposite shore (Mk 8:10). But when we look at the miraculous feedings themselves, we see a much closer resemblance between the miracle narratives, as well as definite dissimilarities. In both feeding accounts, Jesus converses with his disciples before working the miracle, his compassion for the

3

Content	Matthew	Mark	Luke	John
[1] Miracle of Feeding 5,000	14:13-21	6:32-44	9:10b-17	6:1-15
[2] Jesus Walks on Water	14:22-33	6:45-52		6:16-21
Other Miracles-Cures	14:34-36	6:53-56		
[3] Jesus Disputes with Pharisees	15:1-20	7:1-23		
Cure of Woman's Daughter	15:21-28	7:24-30		
[4] Cure of Deaf-Mute (and Others)	(15:29-31)	7:31-37		
[1] Miracle of Feeding 4,000	15:32-38	8:1-9		
[2] Jesus Crosses the Sea	15:39	8:10		
[3] Jesus Disputes with Pharisees	16:1-4	8:11-13		
Leaven of the Pharisees	16:5-12	8:14-21		
[4] Cure of the Blind Man		8:22-26		
Peter's Confession of Christ	16:13-20	8:27-30	9:18-21	6:67-71

crowd is mentioned, there are very few loaves and fishes, the crowd is commanded to sit, Jesus prays over the bread and distributes it through his disciples, and when all have eaten, much is left over and gathered up. But there are differences between these narratives too. In Mark 6, some 5,000 are fed with five loaves and two fishes. In Mark 8, the crowd numbers 4,000 and there are seven loaves and a few fishes.

On the basis of the many similarities in the Gospel's structure at this point and in Mark's description of the incident itself, scholars conclude that we have here one more instance of a twice-told tale, this time within the same Gospel. The various explanations offered for this repetition need not be discussed here. All we need note now is that Mark's description of the miraculous feeding(s) does not reproduce exact details of what transpired then. It is interesting to note, also, that while Matthew, like Mark, has the story twice, Luke and John tell it only once.

(c) Perhaps the clearest instance of differing details is in the story of Bartimaeus. As Mark tells it, Bartimaeus, a blind beggar, was healed by Jesus as he *left* Jericho (Mk 10:46-52). Luke follows Mark in reporting only one blind beggar, but Jesus cures him as Jesus *approaches* Jericho (Lk 18:35-43). Matthew gives no name but makes the one man into *two* blind men (Mt 20:29-34. Matthew even repeats the story! See Mt 9:27-31). Such discrepancies do not argue for exact Gospel reproduction of detail.

(d) Even the words attributed to Jesus himself are recorded differently at times. An important lesson like the Lord's Prayer appears with considerable variation. Compare this prayer as we find it in Matthew with the shorter form of the same prayer in Luke:

Matthew 6:9-13	*Luke 11:2-4*
Our Father in heaven,	Father,
hallowed be your name,	hallowed be your name,
your kingdom come,	your kingdom come.
your will be done	
on earth as it is in heaven.	
Give us today our daily bread,	Give us each day our daily bread.
and forgive us the wrong we have done	Forgive us our sins
as we forgive those who wrong us.	for we too forgive all who do us wrong;
Subject us not to the trial	and subject us not to the trial.
but deliver us from the evil one.	

Should it occur to you to say that Jesus might have given several forms of this prayer at different times, we can move on to the institution of the Eucharist. Here one might expect the words of Jesus to be recorded with absolute fidelity, exactly as he spoke them on that solemn occasion. Instead, the Gospel reports vary, as does the one reference to these words of institution in the letter to the Corinthians. The variations here are not great, but they do exist and show us that the evangelists were not always concerned to repeat Jesus verbatim. Compare the following:

1 Corinthians 11:24-25: [Jesus says] This is my body, which is for you. Do this in remembrance of me. . . . This cup is the new covenant in my blood. Do this, whenever you drink it, in remembrance of me.

Luke 22:19-20: This is my body to be given for you. Do this as a remembrance of me. . . . This cup is the new covenant in my blood, which will be shed for you.

6

Mark 14:22-24: Take this, this is my body. . . .
This is my blood, the blood of the covenant, to
be poured out on behalf of many.

Matthew 26:26-28: Take this and eat it, this my
body. . . . All of you must drink from it, for this
is my blood, the blood of the covenant, to be
poured out in behalf of many for the forgiveness
of sins.

All these examples make it abundantly clear that
the Gospels are not—they were never meant to be—
filmed or taped versions of what took place when Jesus
walked the earth. This is not to say that they lack
history, for it is there. But it is not the history that our
modern reader often expects to find. If not our type of
history, what then? How do experts in the biblical sci-
ences view these precious documents today?

Modern scholarship still affirms the Bible as the
word of God. But today, scholars are more aware that
this word comes to us as mediated through men who
were writing for *their* contemporaries. And we also know
now that the authors who finally put the Gospels into
their present form were not working without helpers,
since they made use of the apostolic labors of their
predecessors. In short, the Gospels are the products of a
fairly long compository process and the work of many
hands. We shall elaborate on this as we proceed, but, for
the moment, listen to what recent writers have to say
about the Gospels. They are:

(1) Documents of history, salvation history. This is a
history understood not as the bare chronicling of mere
facts but a history whose meaning is given to us by those
closest to Jesus and their successors. It is a history which
includes both the fact and its interpretation. For in-

stance, although it is already important for us to learn from the evangelists that Jesus was crucified under Pontius Pilate, when Mark tells us also, through the centurion at the foot of the cross, that "Clearly, this man was the Son of God!", the crucifixion takes on a whole new range of meaning for us.

(2) Documents of faith. The Gospels speak of matters known only through faith and testify to the belief of the early church. This is why the insight we gain from the early church's interpretation of the life and ministry of Jesus Christ in the Gospels is so valuable for us. We have here the testimony of believers contemporaneous with Christ, including those who were with Jesus from the start.

(3) Documents from the church. As we shall see presently, the Gospels grew from the activity of the church in its preaching and teaching the mystery of Christ among us. The Gospels are the product of a sacred tradition; they came into existence as the earliest church transmitted the content of its faith to subsequent generations.

(4) Documents for the church. The Gospels were intended to nourish the faith of those for whom they were written. They served the needs of their times, making the Gospel message contemporaneous and relevant for the Christians of the first century and for any others willing to listen. This does not diminish their value for us today. They still speak to us, but somewhat differently. Now they have a regulatory role in our lives, since they carry us back to the period in which our church, of which they form a constitutive element, was founded.

In reading the Gospels, then, the question to be asked is no longer the merely historical "Did it happen exactly as it is written?" "Did Jesus say precisely that and only that?" but "What is God trying to tell us through the sacred author?" This type of question does not do away with the "Gospel truth"; it shifts our attention to what is the Gospel truth. Some years ago, a snappy song in the musical *Kiss Me Kate* asserted, "I'm always true to you, darling, in my fashion ..." This is how the Gospel truth is to be taken today, in *its* fashion, not in some dry, sterile manner imposed on these ancient documents by modern man.

Shapers of the Gospel

Today it is a truism to say that no man is an island. He is subject to countless influences from all sides and has to react in some way to the pressures put upon him. This is no less true of the very human authors who composed our Gospels. They, too, felt the push and tug of competing influences in their own lives and in the lives of their Christian communities. These various influences shaped the work of the evangelists, who were forced to react to these pressures to make their Gospels relevant. Before we look at the growth of the Gospels themselves, then, it would be useful to take a brief look at the more important of these external stimuli.

(1) *Jewish expectations.* Jesus was born into turbulent times. In the two centuries preceding his birth, revolt and the struggle for self-rule had spread over all the ancient Near East. His own day saw the Jewish people chafing under the yoke of Roman rule. Their traditional land was divided. Galilee (with Peraea) was governed by Herod Antipas (4 B.C.—39 A.D.), son of Herod the Great (37—4 B.C.). Roman prefects (before 37 A.D.) and procurators (after 37 A.D.) ruled in Judea and Samaria (and Idumaea) after the disgrace and deposition of Archelaus (4 B.C.—6 A.D.), another of Herod the Great's sons. In a few short years, a series of particularly corrupt and inept Roman procurators would push the

Jewish people to revolt, bringing on the war (66-74 A.D.) which effectively ended when the Temple at Jerusalem was destroyed in 70 A.D.

At the time, political expectations were also religious expectations. Fanatic Jewish revolutionaries actively sought the Lord's anointed king, a Messiah, who would deliver God's people from the tyrannical foreign yoke and establish Israel in a glory surpassing even that of the ancient kingdom under David and Solomon. Over the years, several candidates presented themselves in this guise, all of them failures. When Jesus was taken and executed as just one more messianic pretender, religious people, both the politically fanatic and the piously praying, would have felt their expectations unmet in him. Who ever heard of a crucified Messiah? Of God's failure?

Some three decades later, in the second half of the first Christian century, Jewish Christians must have felt disappointed again. Where was the triumph of Israel? God had justified Jesus' claim to Messianic authority. But persecution of the church by Rome, hostility from fellow Jews, loss of the Holy City and its Temple in the war—all of these must have seemed a sorry reversal of Messianic hopes.

Mark was the first of the Gospels to give the Cross true perspective, as we shall see, but his lesson needed repetition in subsequent Gospels. Jewish expectations had their answer in God's salvific plan, which did not include a politically restored Jewish kingdom.

(2) *Gentile Conversions.* Christianity swept westward through the Diaspora, the Jewish presence outside Palestine, and on into the Gentile world. As it did, it raised questions. How were these new Christians to be incorporated into Christ? Were they to observe the Mosaic Law in its fullness? If not, what was the status of that imper-

ishable Law of Moses? What would become of it if everyone, or even large numbers, could ignore it?

Voices could be heard from the right: The Law of Moses stands. Jesus himself said so. Of course, we understand it differently from the Pharisees, as he did, but nevertheless the Law remains. Other voices responded from the left: Salvation is open to all: we are all, Jews and Gentiles alike, equal before God. It is not necessary to observe the Law as our Pharisaic brethren would have us believe.

Echoes of this serious conflict within early Christianity and of its eventual resolution may be heard from the pages of Matthew and Luke primarily, but the other evangelists have their own light to shed upon these difficult questions. The conversion of the Gentiles was so large a happening it forced itself upon the Gospels as they took their present shape.

(3) *Delay in the Lord's Return.* Once they finally grasped this stupendous fact—Jesus had returned to life—his disciples were deliriously happy. God had vindicated his prophet! The messianic Lord had risen indeed! Although he had returned to his Father for a time, he would soon come again to institute God's definitive reign upon the earth!

But patient weeks and months turned into impatient years. Where is he? Why does he delay his coming? Have those Christians already dead hoped in vain? What are we, the living, to do in the meantime?

Answers to these and other such questions can be seen in the emphasis Matthew gives to church organization and internal affairs. Luke, too, shows traces of a church adapting its Gospel message to a long wait. John, above all, reassures the church that it is not alone while it waits for Jesus to return. His Holy Spirit was promised to Jesus' disciples, he has come, and he remains with them. Once again, a contemporaneous crisis in the church's life has left its impress on the Gospels.

The Gospels in Gestation

Some scientists trace the origin of our universe to a gigantic initial explosion, a cosmic "big bang." However that may be, it seems certain that the Gospels as literary documents began with one such tremendous proclamation—Jesus lives! Soon after Jesus returned to his Father, the Holy Spirit prompted Peter and his co-apostles to spread this good news abroad. To any who would listen, the apostolic band preached astounding facts. Jesus had been taken by his enemies; he had been crucified; he had died and had been buried. Now he lives again. "This is the Jesus God has raised up, and we are his witnesses" (Acts 2:32), so Peter insisted. A new age had dawned in which those sinners who repented and were baptized in the name of Jesus would receive forgiveness of their sins and the gift of the Holy Spirit (Acts 2:37-39). There was no time for delay in accepting this offer; the new age had already come and with it impending judgment. Peter urged his hearers, "Save yourselves from this generation which has gone astray" (Acts 2:40). The message was simple, direct, and clear. It was sent to Israel, but not to Israel exclusively. "It was to you and your children that the promise was made, and to all those still far off, whom the Lord our God calls" (Acts 2:39).

We can see that under these emergency conditions

there would be no thought of writing an extended biography of Jesus or even of composing elaborate instructions for the faithful. If all were to end soon with Jesus' return, there was no need for such writings. The apostolic group had all it could do to carry its urgent message orally to its countrymen to convince them before the fateful day arrived.

Acts 10 has a particularly good summary of early apostolic preaching as the church began to branch out toward the Gentiles. Note especially in verses 38-40 how the barest outline is given of Jesus' ministry and its sequel. Later, four points of this outline appear as a framework for all four Gospels. There is mention of John the Baptist, of Galilee where Jesus began his work, of Judea and Jerusalem, and of the suffering and death of Jesus and his glorious resurrection.

Acts 10:34-43: Apostolic Preaching—
Peter to Cornelius' House

The Gospel is open to all

34 Peter proceeded to address them in these words: I begin to see how true it is that God shows no partiality.

35 Rather, the man of any nation who fears God and acts uprightly is acceptable to him.

But is first sent to Israel

36 This is the message he has sent to the sons of Israel, the good news of peace proclaimed through Jesus Christ who is Lord of all.

Salvation history

John Baptist
Galilee

37 I take it you know what has been reported all over Judea about Jesus of Nazareth,
—beginning in Galilee with the baptism John preached;

38 —of the way God anointed him with the Holy Spirit and power. He went about doing good works and healing all who were in the grip of the devil, and God was with him.

Judea
Jerusalem

39 —We are witnesses to all that he did in the land of the Jews and in Jerusalem.

15

*Passion-
Resurrection*

40—They killed him, finally, hanging him
on a tree, only to have God raise him
up on the third day and grant that he
be seen,

41—not by all, but only by such witnesses as
had been chosen beforehand by God—by
us who ate and drank with him after he
rose from the dead.

*Apostolic
Mission*

42 He commissioned us to preach to the people
and to bear witness that he is the one set
apart by God as judge of the living and the
dead.

*Use of the Old
Testament*

43 To him all the prophets testify, saying that
everyone who believes in him has
forgiveness of sins through his name.

Since assertion is better aided by argument, apostolic testimony was enriched by appeal to the Scriptures, particularly to answer the thorny question of how a Messiah could be truly God's elect and yet be crucified. It was natural to appeal to the holy writings, since all parties in Judaism at the time approached the scriptures to find in them the manifest will of God for the present moment. Peter and the church around him declared that whatever had happened to Jesus had its adequate explanation in the plan of God which lay hidden in the scriptures but which could now be seen.

Opponents of Jesus would argue from Deuteronomy 21:22-23, "If a man guilty of a capital offense is put to death and his corpse hung on a tree, it shall not remain on the tree overnight. You shall bury it the same day; otherwise, since God's curse rests on him who hangs on a tree, you will defile the land which the Lord, your God, is giving you as an inheritance." How, then, could this Jesus who was executed as a messianic pretender be the Christ of God? The holy Law itself held him accursed by God. Paul turned this text around to give it a positive meaning. Jesus was innocent, but he had died on our behalf. Paul wrote, "Christ has delivered us from the power of the law's curse by himself becoming a curse for us, as it is written: 'Accursed is anyone who is hanged on a tree' " (Gal 3:13).

This picture of an innocent Jesus, whose suffering was foreseen and became part of the divine redemptive plan, could be better illustrated by texts from Isaiah. Jesus was the Servant of God mentioned in Isaiah 52:13 —53:12, an innocent sufferer now vindicated by God (see Acts 3:13-15). We can see how the church envisioned Jesus by looking at the text of Isaiah.

Isaiah 52:13—53:12

See, my servant shall prosper,
he shall be raised high and greatly exalted.
Even as many were amazed at him—
so marred was his look beyond that of man,
and his appearance beyond that of mortals—
So shall he startle many nations,
because of him kings shall stand speechless;
For those who have not been told shall see,
those who have not heard shall ponder it.
Who would believe what we have heard?
To whom has the arm of the Lord been revealed?
He grew up like a sapling before him,
like a shoot from the parched earth;
There was in him no stately bearing to make us
   look at him,
nor appearance that would attract us to him.
He was spurned and avoided by men,
a man of suffering, accustomed to infirmity,
One of those from whom men hide their faces,
spurned, and we held him in no esteem.
Yet it was our infirmities that he bore,

17

our sufferings that he endured,
While we thought of him as stricken,
as one smitten by God and afflicted.
But he was pierced for our offenses,
crushed for our sins,
Upon him was the chastisement that makes us
   whole,
by his stripes we were healed.
We had all gone astray like sheep,
each following his own way;
But the Lord laid upon him
the guilt of us all.
Though he was harshly treated, he submitted
and opened not his mouth;
Like a lamb led to the slaughter
or a sheep before the shearers,
he was silent and opened not his mouth.
Oppressed and condemned, he was taken away,
and who would have thought any more of his
   destiny?
When he was cut off from the land of the living,
and smitten for the sin of his people,
A grave was assigned him among the wicked
and a burial place with evildoers,
Though he had done no wrong
nor spoken any falsehood.
[But the Lord was pleased
to crush him in infirmity.]
If he gives his life as an offering for sin,
he shall see his descendants in a long life,
and the will of the Lord shall be accomplished
   through him.
Because of his affliction
he shall see the light in fullness of days;

Through his suffering; my servant shall justify
    many,
and their guilt he shall bear.
Therefore I will give him his portion among the
    great,
and he shall divide the spoils with the mighty,
Because he surrendered himself to death
and was counted among the wicked;
And he shall take away the sins of many,
and win pardon for their offenses.

This Isaiah passage left its imprint on the Gospels.
Note the echoes of it and other prophetic passages in
what is told about the suffering of Jesus.

(1) The Arrest of Jesus

Isaiah 53:6
We had all gone astray like sheep,
each following his own way;
But the Lord laid upon him
the guilt of us all.

Zechariah 13:7
Strike the shepherd that the sheep
    may be dispersed.

Mark 14:50
All deserted him and fled.

(2) Jesus on Trial

Isaiah 53:7
Though he was harshly treated, he submitted
and opened not his mouth;

Like a lamb led to the slaughter
or a sheep before the shearers,
he was silent and opened not his mouth.

Mark 14:60-61; 15:4-5

The high priest rose to his feet before the court
and began to interrogate Jesus: "Have you no
answer to what these men testify against you?"
But Jesus remained silent; he made no reply...
Pilate interrogated him again; "Surely you have
some answer? See how many accusations they
are leveling against you?" But greatly to Pilate's
surprise, Jesus made no further response.

(3) **Jesus Mistreated at the Time of the Trials**

Isaiah 50:6
I gave my back to those who beat me,
my cheeks to those who plucked my beard;
My face I did not shield
from buffets and spitting.

Mark 14:65; 15:16-19
Some of them then began to spit on him. They
blindfolded him and hit him, saying, "Play the
prophet!" ... The soldiers now led Jesus away
into the hall known as the praetorium; at the
same time they assembled the whole cohort ...
Continually striking Jesus on the head with a
reed and spitting at him, they genuflected before
him and pretended to pay him homage.

(4) Jesus Crucified with Two Insurgents

Isaiah 53:12
. . .he surrendered himself to death
and was counted among the wicked;
And he shall take away the sins of many,
and win pardon for their offenses.

Mark 15:27
With him they crucified two insurgents, one at his
right and one at his left.

Jesus hung on the cross for a considerable portion of
that fateful day. Recalling that time, the earliest narra-
tors of the Passion could have said much about his
reactions, those of the bystanders, the passersby, and the
soldiers charged with the execution. You can see, however, where the interest of the early church actually lay.
It keeps the story simple and direct, selecting only those
features of this painful period that it found foreshadowed in the scriptures and narrating very little else.
Compare the final moments of Jesus as described in
Mark 15:22-41 with these passages from the Psalms,
particularly Psalm 22.

Mark 15:22-41	*Psalms*
22 When they brought Jesus to the site of Golgotha (which means "Skull Place"),	
23 they tried to give him wine drugged with myrrh, but he would not take it.	69:22 . . .in my thirst they gave me vinegar to drink.
24 Then they crucified him and divided up his garments by rolling dice for them to see what each should take.	22:19 they divide my garments among them, and for my vesture they cast lots.

25 It was about nine in the morning when they crucified him.

26 The inscription proclaiming his offense read, "The King of the Jews."

27 With him they crucified two insurgents, one at his right and one at his left.

29 People going by kept insulting him, tossing their heads and saying, "Ha, ha! So you were going to destroy the temple and rebuild it in three days!

30 Save yourself now by coming down from that cross!"

31 The chief priests and the scribes also joined in and jeered: "He saved others but he cannot save himself!

32 Let the 'Messiah,' the 'king of Israel,' come down from that cross here and now so that we can see it and believe in him!" The men who had been crucified with him likewise kept taunting him.

33 When noon came, darkness fell on the whole countryside and lasted until midafternoon.

34 At that time Jesus cried in a loud voice, "*Eloi, Eloi, lama sabachthani?*" which means, "My God, my God, why have you forsaken me?"

22:18 They look on and gloat over me.

22:8 All who see me scoff at me; they mock me with parted lips, they wag their heads;

22:9 He relied on the Lord; let him deliver him, let him rescue him if he loves him.

22:1 My God, my God, why have you forsaken me?

35 A few of the bystanders who heard it remarked, "Listen! He is calling on Elijah!"

36 Someone ran off, and soaking a sponge in sour wine, stuck it on a reed to try to make him drink. The man said, "Now let's see whether Elijah comes to take him down."

69:22 . . . in my thirst they gave me vinegar to drink

37 Then Jesus, uttering a loud cry, breathed his last.

38 At that moment the curtain in the sanctuary was torn in two from top to bottom.

39 The centurion who stood guard over him, on seeing the manner of his death, declared, "Clearly this man was the Son of God!"

40 There were also women present looking on from a distance. Among them were Mary Magdalene, Mary the mother of James the younger and Joses, and Salome.

38:12 My friends and my companions stand back because of my affliction; my neighbors stand afar off.

41 These women had followed Jesus when he was in Galilee and attended to his needs. There were also many others who had come up with him to Jerusalem.

Terribly important though it was, the difficulty of a crucified Messiah was not the only one the early church had to face. As the church grew, many questions arose.

How did Jesus answer the Pharisees and the Sadducees? How are we to do this? What did Jesus say about taxes, about Gentiles, about the Roman authorities? What significance does baptism have for us? Or the Lord's supper? How are we to act toward one another? Tell us something of the life of Jesus. What did he do? What did he say?

Gradually, over the years, these various needs, polemical, social, liturgical, communitarian, and even biographical, had to be met. Bit by bit, the material was assembled. Constant repetition forced it into set patterns and literary categories. There were miracle stories telling how Jesus had advanced the kingdom of God by healing those under the influence of Satan. There were parables, too, in which Jesus imparted many important lessons, like the necessity of being forgiving of others. His relationship with certain towns and cities, notably Nazareth, Capernaum, Bethsaida, Chorazin, and Jerusalem, were made public record for the church. His conflicts with scribes of various persuasions were recorded.

Similar items were collected into units, and some of these collections can be seen today in our Gospels. Various criteria organized the subject matter and formed the collections. For instances, look at the way these items have been put together.

(1) Organization around scriptural texts.

We have already seen how selection of events from the prolonged suffering and death of Jesus was partially determined by resemblances to Psalm 22, which was seen to foreshadow the death of the Lord. Later on, Luke 1—2 was arranged so as to allude to Malachi 3:1, "Lo, I am sending my messenger to prepare the way before me; and suddenly there will come to the temple the Lord whom you seek, and the messenger of the covenant whom you desire." Luke speaks first of the annunciation of John the Baptist's birth, then of the annunciation of Jesus. He tells of the birth of the Baptist, then that of Jesus. He closes these two chapters with Jesus in the Temple, first as a baby, then as a twelve-year-old. In so constructing these two chapters, Luke reminds his readers that John the Baptist was the expected Elijah, the forerunner of the Christ.

(2) Organization around subject matter.

Mark 2:1—3:6 contains a series of strife stories, in which Jesus clashes with opponents, notably the Pharisees. At the end of this series, the conclusion is reached: "When the Pharisees went outside, they immediately began to plot with the Herodians how they might destroy him."

Mark 4 contains a series of parables whose basic imagery is agricultural. Matthew 13 also contains a collection of parables.

(3) Organization around a theme.

Luke 11:14-26 pits the kingdom of God (as evidenced in the work of Jesus) against the kingdom of Satan. A series of sayings—a,b,c,d—which appear to have been independent originally carry this theme.

(a) *The accusation: Jesus expels demons by Satan's power.*
Jesus was casting out a devil which was mute, and when the devil was cast out the dumb man spoke. The crowds were amazed at this. Some of them said, "It is by Beelzebul, the prince of devils, that he casts out devils." Others, to test him, were demanding a sign from heaven.

The response: Satan does not war with himself.
Expelling demons is God's work, whoever does it.

Because he knew their thoughts, he said to
them, "Every kingdom divided against itself is
laid waste. Any house torn by dissension falls. If
Satan is divided against himself, how can his
kindgom last?—since you say it is by Beelzebul
that I cast out devils. If I cast out devils by
Beelzebul, by whom do your people cast them
out? In such case, let them act as your judges.
But if it is by the finger of God that I cast out
devils, then the reign of God is upon you.

(b) *God is stronger than Satan, so Jesus can cast*
out demons. ("Beelzebul" means "Lord of the
house," suggesting this imagery.)
When a strong man fully armed guards his
courtyard, his possessions go undisturbed. But
when someone stronger than he comes and
overpowers him, such a one carries off the arms
on which he was relying and divides the spoils.

(c) *One must take sides in the struggle between*
Jesus and Satan.
He who is not with me is against me, and he
who does not gather with me scatters.

(d) *Relapse into Satan's power is an evil to be*
avoided.
When an unclean spirit has gone out of a man,
it wanders through arid wastes searching for a
resting-place; failing to find one, it says, "I will
go back to where I came from." It then returns,
to find the house swept and tidied. Next it goes
out and returns with seven other spirits far
worse than itself, who enter in and dwell there.

The result is that the last state of the man is
worse than the first.

(4) Organization around catch-words.

Here one word seems to suggest another (as
"Beelzebul," "Lord of the house," suggested the saying
on the strong man and his house in the previous example). Mark 9:42-50 (here taken from the Revised Stan-
dard Version, which approximates the Greek text more
closely) illustrates this type of grouping.

> *Mark 9:42-50*: Whoever *causes* one of these little
> ones who believe in me *to sin*, it would be better
> for him if a great millstone were hung around
> his neck and he were thrown into the sea. And
> if your hand *causes* you *to sin*, cut it off; it is
> better for you to enter life maimed than with
> two hands to go to hell, to the unquenchable
> fire. And if your foot *causes* you *to sin,* cut it off;
> it is better for you to enter life lame than with
> two feet to be thrown into hell. And if your eye
> *causes* you *to sin*, pluck it out; it is better for you
> to enter the kingdom of God with one eye than
> with two eyes to be thrown into hell, where the
> worm does not die, and the *fire* is not quenched.
> For everyone will be *salted* with *fire. Salt* is
> good; but if the *salt* has lost its *saltness*, how
> will you season it? Have *salt* in yourselves, and
> be at peace with one another.

As the church grew and spread out more and more
into the Mediterranean world, access to those who had
been in direct contact with the Lord or his immediate
discipleship became increasingly impossible. Death
claimed the earliest Christians one by one. It is not

surprising, then, that, before long, attempts were made to embody the teaching of, and about, Jesus Christ in some sort of written form. Luke tells us of these early attempts in the preface to his own Gospel.

> *Luke 1:1-4*: Many have undertaken to compile a narrative of the events which have been fulfilled in our midst, precisely as those events were transmitted to us by the original eyewitnesses and ministers of the word. I too have carefully traced the whole sequence of events from the beginning, and have decided to set it in writing for you, Theophilus, so that your Excellency may see how reliable the instruction was that you received.

The Gospels as we know them were about to appear. Before we investigate them individually, however, pause a moment to reflect on the process we have just seen. The community of believers has taken the apostolic witness, the teaching about Jesus Christ and derived from Jesus Christ, and has put it into such memorable forms as would aid the instruction of the faithful. At what point writing entered the process we do not know, but the end result of this long transmission of the material was the setting down of the Gospel of Jesus Christ according to one or other author, according to Matthew, Mark, Luke or John.

Three stages, then, are present in the composition of each of our Gospels: (1) the ministry of Jesus of Nazareth, (2) the interpretation of the Lord Jesus and his ministry in the early church, and (3) the specific emphases of the individual evangelists. We can summarize what we know already in the accompanying chart.

Stages in the Growth of the Gospels

I *The Ministry of Jesus.*
Jesus announces and brings the kingdom of God by his teaching and his miracles.

II. *The Interpretation of Jesus and His Ministry in the Earliest Church.*

A. Apostolic Testimony and Preaching.
—God has raised up Jesus and made him Lord.
—historical outline: John the Baptist, Galilee, Judea (Jerusalem), Passion-Resurrection

B. Further Teaching Answering the Needs of a Growing Community.
—apologetic —how could the Messiah be crucified?
—polemic —how did Jesus answer the Pharisees and Sadducees?
—spiritual —how is one to live to gain the Kingdom of Heaven?
—social —what about taxes, enemies, sinners, Romans?
—liturgical —what is the significance of Baptism? the Eucharist?
—biographical —tell us something about Jesus' life and background.

This teaching was at first oral, was selective, historical, theological, schematic, and gradually fixed. It made free use of the scriptures. It grouped materials on various principles.

C. Early Attempts at Gospel Writings.
—noted in the preface to Luke's Gospel.

III. *The Evangelists' Emphases on the Tradition.*
Mark: Who Is This Man Jesus?—The Suffering Servant and Son of God.
Matthew: A People Renewed
Luke: Good News for *Everybody!*
John: Divinity Among Us.

Just Who Is This Man Jesus?
The Gospel of Mark

Who wrote our first Gospel? Most scholars today will answer that Mark did. But who is Mark? The Acts of the Apostles, our earliest church history, tells us that he was a Jerusalemite, "John also known as Mark" (Acts 12:12), whose mother, Mary, was apparently a well-to-do-widow, since John Mark's father never appears and her house was large enough to have a maid and to be the gathering place for Christians (Acts 12:12-13).

Later on in Acts, when Paul and Barnabas complete their famine relief visit to Jerusalem, we see them recruit John Mark for the missions and take him back to Antioch (Turkish Antakya, on the eastern Mediterranean coast, Acts 12:25). Mark then joined their expedition to evangelize Cyprus (Acts 13:5) and accompanied them to Perge in Pamphylia (on the southern coast of Turkey). There, Mark left his mentors (Acts 13:13). The circumstances of this departure must not have been pleasant, because Paul flatly refused to take Mark along the next time an expedition was planned (Acts 15:37-39). Mark split Paul and Barnabas, but Paul was later reconciled to Mark, calling Mark his "fellow-worker" (Philemon 24) and asking the Colossians to make Mark welcome (Col 4:10). Later yet, 2 Timothy 4:11 expects Mark to be of great service to Paul in the latter's captivity.

Significantly, Mark is also seen as the associate of Peter, who calls him "my son Mark" (1 Pet 5:13). Subsequent tradition links Mark with Peter in his Roman apostolate. This pairing turned out to be most significant for the composition of Mark's Gospel, which is generally placed at Rome. The date of Mark's Gospel is not clearly determinable. Conflicting testimony from ancient writers put it both before and after Peter's Roman martyrdom in the mid 60's of the first Christian century. Most scholars agree, however, that Mark is the first of our canonical or normative Gospels.

When Mark set out to compose his Gospel, he was not starting from scratch. He had, as we have seen, apostolic testimony to the resurrection of Jesus Christ and a basic outline of the Lord's earthly ministry. The beginning of the Gospel of Jesus Christ lay in the work of John the Baptist, who preached repentance (Mk 1:1-4) and baptized Jesus (Mk 1:9-11; see Acts 1:21-22). After John's arrest, Jesus preached the Gospel of God in Galilee—repent, believe! (Mk 1:14-15). Eventually, Jesus moved through Galilee heading for Jerusalem (Mk 9:30; 10:1, 32; 11:1, 11), where he suffered, died, was buried, and was raised from the dead (Mk 14—16).

In addition to this traditional outline, Mark had years of pastoral instruction in the faith to utilize. Portions of this teaching had already received a fixed form; some of it was already gathered into blocks of materials suitable for conveying one or other point of early Christian teaching. You can see in Mark, as we have noted, a collection of parables with an agricultural theme (Mk 4:1-20, 26-29, 30-32) and a group of strife stories in which Jesus clashes with his opponents, principally Pharisees, over questions of the Law's observance (Mk 2:1—3:6).

Association with Peter probably provided Mark with even more material, some of it quite personal for Peter, as the cure of his mother-in-law (Mk 1:29-31) or Peter's denials of Jesus (Mk 14:66-72).

By now, identification of Jesus as the suffering Servant depicted by the prophet Isaiah had taken firm root in the developing tradition. It went side by side with identification of Jesus as Messiah. Jesus was even a suffering Messiah! He was also the persecuted, innocent man of Psalm 22. Early accounts of his death had already been formed around these themes.

Mark took up his traditional material and organized it so as to show that the nature of Jesus' messiahship went against the expectations of all who were close to him. They did not perceive the true import of Jesus and his mission until after his resurrection. It was hidden from them by their own obtuseness, and yet it was there before them all the time. Others, too, missed it, particularly those who were not at all morally disposed to receive the teaching of Jesus. It was as if one gigantic secret confronted them all, which only the events of the Passion and Resurrection would disclose. True, Jesus was Lord, and he was the expected Messiah of Israel, but the realization of Israel's expectations had turned out to be so different!

Of course, Jesus' disciples would not have been his followers at all had they not been sufficiently well disposed to receive Jesus when he came among them. That is why Peter, aided by God's grace, would eventually penetrate to the fact that Jesus was Messiah. Mark makes Peter's identification the pivotal point of Mark's Gospel. Before Peter's confession that Jesus is the Christ (Mk 8:27-30), the personality of Jesus is shrouded in mystery. After Peter's affirmation, when the disciples have come to realize just who Jesus is, the newly identified Messiah introduces them to a sadder aspect of his messianic reality: he is to suffer before being glorified. In time, his disciples will walk the same path, and so Jesus is not only their leader, he is their model.

Look now at how Mark develops this teaching. Jesus, unlike the scribes the people usually hear, teaches authoritatively in the synagogue at Capernaum (Mk 1:21-22). This causes all who hear him to wonder, not at what he says, for Mark does not give us the content of this preaching, but at the way Jesus teaches, as one with authority. "What is this? A new teaching with authority!" (Mk 1:27). Already Mark hints at the mystery of Jesus' personality.

The miracle which then takes place identifies Jesus, for the unclean spirit about to be expelled shrieks, "I know who you are—the holy one of God" (Mk 1:24). Jesus, however, does not need the testimony of demons, so he silences the unclean spirit (Mk 1:25). This too causes the crowd to wonder. He not only teaches authoritatively, he also commands the obedience of unclean spirits (Mk 1:27).

Again in Mark 1:34 and 3:11-12 (see 5:6-7), Jesus muzzles the malevolent spirits. Stranger still, he gives a stern warning to a leper he cures, "Say nothing to anyone" (Mk 1:44), tells Jairus and his wife not to let anyone know that Jesus has brought their daughter back to life (with a crowd present in the house!) (Mk 5:43), tries unsuccessfully to impose silence after curing a deaf man (Mk 7:36), and forbids a blind man whose sight has been restored to enter his own village (Mk 8:26). He tries to hide (Mk 7:24; 9:30) but cannot (Mk 7:24). He has stirred up too much excitement and wonder, even awe. "We have never seen anything like this!" (Mk 2:12). "Who is this? Even the wind and the sea obey him!" (Mk 4:41).

In one instance only does Jesus encourage someone

to proclaim a cure. But this preaching takes place throughout the Decapolis, a league of some ten cities predominantly Gentile in population and sympathy. Jewish political aspirations would not find support here. Here it would be safe to tell all about the cure wrought by Jesus (Mk 5:18-20). Note, however, that the imposition of silence on the deaf-mute also occurs in the Decapolis (Mk 7:31-37). Some scholars explain that Mark's geography in verse 31 is confused, but perhaps Jesus was only on the fringes of the Decapolis at this point and so still among a population largely Jewish.

Obviously, one who commands the elements and loosens the grip Satan has on the world must be the Messiah. Peter gladly acknowledges this:

> *Mark 8:27-30*: Then Jesus and his disciples set out for the villages around Caesarea Philippi. On the way he asked his disciples this question: "Who do people say that I am?" They replied, "Some, John the Baptizer, others, Elijah, still others, one of the prophets." "And you," he went on to ask, "who do you say that I am?" Peter answered him, "You are the Messiah!" Then he gave them strict orders not to tell anyone about him.

Peter and the other disciples are placed under strict orders not to reveal Jesus' identity until he has risen from the dead (Mk 8:30; 9:9). Mark has one eye on Roman authorities as he narrates Jesus' story. Jesus was not a political Messiah, despite the expectations of the crowds and even of the disciples. Rome had nothing to fear from him politically. The charge Pilate formulated against Jesus—king of the Jews—was false from the political standpoint. And yet how true from another!

The Gospel of Mark

Once Mark has Peter acknowledge Jesus as the Messiah, the designation appears more often in Mark's Gospel. Apart from its use in the title of the book (Mk 1:1), "Messiah" ("Christ" in the Greek original of Mark) appears only after the pivotal point of Peter's messianic identification of Jesus, in Mk 8:20; 9:41; 12:35; 13:21; 14:61; 15:32. The question of Messiahship takes on greater importance: Who is he? Where is he?

Jesus, Peter tells us, is Messiah. But what type of Messiah? Mark prepares the reader for a new understanding of messiahship by having Jesus predict his own doom immediately after Peter has acknowledged him. Jesus repeats this passion prediction two times in Mark, the last time in a most detailed fashion:

Mark 8:31: "He began to teach them that the Son of Man had to suffer much, be rejected by the elders, the chief priests, and the scribes, be put to death, and rise three days later."

Mark 9:31: "He was teaching his disciples in this vein, 'The Son of Man is going to be delivered into the hands of men who will put him to death; three days after his death he will rise.'"

Mark 10:32-34: "Taking the Twelve aside once more, he began to tell them what was going to happen to him. 'We are on our way up to Jerusalem, where the Son of Man will be handed over to the chief priests and the scribes. They will condemn him to death and hand him over to the Gentiles, who will mock him and spit at him, flog him, and finally kill him. But three days later he will rise.'"

35

One might wonder why, after so detailed a prediction from Jesus' own lips, the disciples would not have been sitting at the door of Jesus' tomb on that first Easter Sunday waiting for the promised resurrection. The answer, of course, is that the threefold repetition and the amount of precise detail in these predictions are the work of the evangelist himself. Mark wants to contrast the explicit forecasting of Jesus' impending suffering with a very obvious lack of understanding on the part of Jesus' disciples. Each time that Mark has the newly discovered Messiah predict his own demise in a flood of suffering, Mark also notes how the disciples disappoint the Master. After the first Passion prediction, Peter tries to dissuade Jesus from following through the divine plan (Mk 8:32-33). After the second, Mark includes the disciples' argument over their own relative importance (Mk 9:33-35). After the third, James and John grow ambitious for preferred places in the kingdom to come (Mk 10:35-45).

> *Mark 8:32-33:* "He said these things quite openly. Peter then took him aside and began to remonstrate with him. At this he turned around and, eyeing the disciples, reprimanded Peter: 'Get out of my sight, you satan! You are not judging by God's standards but by man's!' "

> *Mark 9:33-35:* "They returned to Capernaum and Jesus, once inside the house, began to ask them, 'What were you discussing on the way home?' At this they fell silent, for on the way they had been arguing about who was the most important. So he sat down and called the twelve around him and said, 'If anyone wishes to rank first, he must remain the last one of all and the servant of all.' "

Mark 10:35-45: "Zebedee's sons, James and John, approached him. 'Teacher,' they said, 'we want you to grant our request.' 'What is it?' he asked. They replied, 'See to it that we sit, one at your right and the other at your left, when you come into your glory.' Jesus told them, 'You do not know what you are asking. Can you drink the cup I shall drink or be baptized in the same bath of pain as I?' 'We can,' they told him. Jesus said in response, 'From the cup I drink of you shall drink; the bath I am immersed in you shall share. But as for sitting at my right or my left, that is not mine to give; it is for those to whom it has been reserved.' The other ten, on hearing this, became indignant at James and John. Jesus called them together and said to them: 'You know how among the Gentiles those who seem to exercise authority lord it over them; their great ones make their importance felt. It cannot be like that with you. Anyone among you who aspires to greatness must serve the rest; whoever wants to rank first among you must serve the needs of all. The Son of Man has not come to be served but to serve—to give his life in ransom for the many.' "

This last statement gives us another important aspect of Mark's thought. Jesus, whose royalty is nowhere proclaimed more openly than in the narrative of his suffering (Mk 15:2, 9, 12, 17-18, 26, 32) abases himself for the service of his brethren. Thus, Jesus is a model for his church. Mark's lesson makes even more sense at a time when persecution is making it cost something to belong to Christ. Persecution allows the Christian to follow Jesus on his path through suffering to glory. If Mark's

Stages in the Growth of the Gospels (2)

I. The Ministry of Jesus

II. The Interpretation of Jesus and His Ministry in the Earliest Church
(Mark's Source Material:)
  —apostolic witness to Jesus as Risen Lord
  —traditional outline of Jesus' ministry: John the Baptist, Galilee, Judea (Jerusalem), Passion-Resurrection.
  —collected materials: e.g., strife stories, parables, sayings.
  —Petrine memories: e.g., curing of Peter's mother-in-law.

III. The Evangelists' Emphases on the Tradition
A. Mark
(Mark's Sources)

6:32:8:26 miracles of feeding crowd, etc.
9:30 journey through Galilee
9:42-50 collection of catch-word sayings
10:1 journey to Judea
11:1, 11 Jerusalem
14-15 Passion of Jesus
16 Resurrection of Christ

4:1-34 collection of parables
2:1-3:6 strife stories
1:29-31 cure of Peter's mother-in-law
1:14 Galilee
1:2-8 John the Baptist

Mark

15:39 Centurion: this man was the Son of God
10:35-45 James and John are ambitious
10:32-34 third passion prediction
9:33-35 the disciples dispute over greatness
9:31 second passion prediction
9:7 God: this is my son, my beloved, listen to him
8:32-33 Peter dissuades Jesus
8:31 first passion prediction
8:27-30 Peter: You are the Messiah!
7:37 He has done everything well!
6:15b others: Jesus is a prophet
6:15a others: Jesus is Elijah
6:14-16 Herod: Jesus is John the Baptist risen
6:2 synagogue audience: Where did he get all this?
5:6-7 possessed man: Jesus, Son of God Most High
4:41 Who can this be that the wind and the sea obey him?
3:11 unclean spirits: You are the Son of God
1:34 the demons: they knew him
1:24 unclean spirit: ... you are—the holy One of God
1:11 heavenly voice: You are my beloved Son

(Mark's Emphasis)

Roman community does not understand this, they need only look at the Twelve, who also did not understand at first.

The recurring theme of Mark's Gospel, then, is the true identity of Jesus Christ. He was the Messiah from the beginning of his ministry (Mk 1:1) but not the Messiah of popular expectations. His teaching and marvelous deeds spoke more eloquently of him than public pretensions could have. The facts identified him. But even when Jesus' disciples saw this, they had more to learn. The true nature of Jesus' Lordship was in humble service of others. Humiliation was the path to glory. It took a pagan soldier in the hire of Rome to perceive the significance of Jesus. "The centurion who stood guard over him, on seeing the manner of his death, declared, 'Clearly, this man *was* the Son of God!' " (Mk 15:39). What was the manner of his death? How did Jesus die? In the service of others.

Mark makes Jesus emphasize the lesson. "He summoned the crowd with his disciples and said to them: 'If a man wishes to come after me, he must deny his very self, take up his cross, and follow in my steps' " (Mk 8:34).

Since we do not have Mark's sources before us today but must discover them by literary analysis of his Gospel and other New Testament writings, it is often difficult to detect where the sources left off and Mark's work begins. In the following chart, the roots of Mark's Gospel are indicated in sections I and II. In section III, *some* of what Mark received from the tradition is shown above the line. Other passages, perhaps also received from the tradition much as they appear, are cited below the line, because they illustrate how Mark emphasizes the identity of Jesus as messianic Son of God and Suffering Servant.

A People Renewed
The Gospel of Matthew

The name of Matthew appears in the select group of the Twelve closest to Jesus (Mk 3:18; Mt 10:3; Lk 6:15; Acts 1:13) and again in the call of the tax-collector Matthew to follow Jesus (Mt 9:9). Mark and Luke have a similar story of a tax-collector's vocation to follow Jesus, but they identify him as Levi, son of Alphaeus (Mk 2:14; Lk 5:27, 29). While scholars have lingering doubts whether Matthew and Levi are the one man, it has been usual since antiquity to identify the two. Double names, sometimes both of them Semitic, are not unknown in biblical times. Judas Maccabee and his four brothers all have two names (1 Maccabees 2:2-5), and in the New Testament, there are Simon/Peter (also known as Cephas) (Jn 1:42), Saul/Paul (Acts 13:9), John/Mark (Acts 12:12), Joseph Bar Sabbas/Justus (Acts 1:23), and Jesus/Justus (Colossians 4:11).

Eusebius, a fourth-century bishop, quotes Papias, a second-century bishop: "Matthew collected the oracles in the Hebrew language and each individual interpreted them as best he could." For years, scholars have argued over this very vague statement, their appreciation of it going all the way from outright rejection of it to acceptance of it as meaning that our present Gospel of Matthew was first written in Hebrew (which they take to mean Aramaic, the language then spoken widely in Palestine) and then translated.

Whatever the value of Papias' statement, contemporary research on the Gospels makes it abundantly clear that our present Gospel of Matthew was not written by the apostle of that name. The basic reason for saying this lies in the Gospels' long compository process and particularly in the evident dependence of Matthew on Mark's Gospel. Why, if Matthew were present to the events he relates, should he, an apostle and eyewitness, have needed Mark, who was neither an apostle nor eyewitness, as a source for his own work? Why use Mark? And yet it is obvious that Mark lies before the author of Matthew's Gospel as he composes. It is not far afield to call Matthew a revised and expanded edition of Mark, provided that we keep in mind that Matthew is an author in his own right, with his own point of view, as the revisions and expansions demonstrate.

Two examples will suffice here to illustrate Matthew's dependence on Mark. (1) Matthew 8:16 says that as evening drew on "they" brought Jesus many who were possessed and that he expelled the demons with a single word and cured the sick. In the parallel passage, Mark 1:32, the reference to the evening is explained by the fact that Mark has been describing a Sabbath day, on which Jews were not to work (Mk 1:21). Not being permitted to carry burdens on the Sabbath, even if these burdens were their own sick, the healthy waited till sunset, when the Sabbath was officially over, to approach Jesus with their sick. Matthew's reference to evening has no adequate explanation in his own Gospel, since he has omitted any reference to the Sabbath here. His mention of bringing the sick in the evening can only be explained by supposing he has been following Mark's order of events down to the Sabbath situation in Mk 1:21, has inserted the Sermon on the Mount (Mt 4:23—7:29) where Mark makes mention of Jesus' teaching with authority (Mk 1:22, see Mt 7:29), and in resuming Mark's sequence with the cure of Peter's mother-in-law, neglects to remove the reference to "evening" when he reached Mk 1:32. He copies it without adverting to the fact that he has not previously mentioned a Sabbath to explain the wait till evening.

(2) In Mark 2:1-12, Jesus cures a paralyzed man. The four who carried this man went to considerable trouble to set him before Jesus. The crowds at Jesus' door prevented entry there, so the bearers took the poor man up onto the roof, opened a hole in it, and lowered the sick man down inside the room where Jesus taught. Mark tells us that "when Jesus saw their faith," he cured the paralytic. Matthew 9:1-8, in repeating this story, omits all reference to the bearers' difficulty and its solution and simply says, "when Jesus saw their faith," he cured the sick man. Why Jesus should focus on the faith of the bearers and not that of the paralytic (possibly barely conscious) becomes clearer if we realize that Matthew has the text of Mark before him as he writes.

These and other instances (and arguments) support the conclusion that Mark was primary source material for the evangelist Matthew. If so, scholars contend, the author of this Gospel is not likely one of the Twelve closest to Jesus.

Because Matthew's Gospel is so deeply concerned with Judaism and Jewish affairs, scholars today generally localize its composition in Syria-Palestine. No further precision seems possible at the moment. Matthew probably achieved its final form as our present Gospel somewhere in the last quarter of the first Christian century.

If Mark's Gospel had reached Matthew's locality, it must have been a success. Why then did Matthew write? Because each community has its own needs. Successful though Mark was in Italy some years earlier, Matthew found that the earlier Gospel did not fully meet the demands placed upon his church or say all that would be useful for it. Building upon Mark in his own locality, Matthew put together an expanded Gospel message which included such revisions and additions as would make the Gospel relevant where he worked.

Taking over most of Mark's Gospel for his own, Matthew inevitably incorporated traditional material into his new work. From apostolic preaching, he derived, through Mark, the primitive witness to the resurrection of Christ and the basic outline of Jesus' ministry. From the later development of apostolic teaching, Matthew obtained those lesser unities—strife stories, parables, sayings, and so on—which Mark had used in his Gospel.

More importantly, Matthew picked up large elements of Markan theology. He could not avoid this, did not want to, and even elaborated upon particular points of this theology, since it reflected a common Christian tradition. Even Mark's twofold division of the ministry of Jesus, which pivots on Peter's profession of faith in Jesus as the Messiah, finds echo in Matthew. The phrase, "From that time on, Jesus began to . . ." appears twice in Matthew (Mt 4:17; 16:21). In Matthew 4:17, it begins the narration of Jesus' early ministry, the period preceding Peter's act of faith. In Matthew 16:21, immediately after Peter's proclamation of Jesus as Messiah, the phrase initiates the road to the Cross. Thus the phrase, although Matthean, echoes the Markan structure and theology. A similar phrase, "from that time on, he [Judas] sought . . ." precedes the Last Supper and the events of the Passion-Resurrection narratives, another major division in Mark's work. Other elements of Mark taken over into Matthew include the three Passion predictions and their disappointing apostolic sequels.

Most of Mark's theology, then, was acceptable to Matthew and now forms elements of his own. But Matthew wanted to improve upon Mark. Why? There was need to. As time passed on, those who could supplement the Gospel of Mark with their own reminiscences had also passed on. But they left behind a legacy of materials, largely sayings, that Matthew thought should be preserved. The Lord's delay in returning meant that his church would be here for some time to come, and so it was important to have his views on many things. Also, the church needed further instruction about its internal affairs and discipline. Most important of all, it was necessary to relate the church of Jesus Christ to the community of Israel which increasingly did not accept him and to guide the Christian's attitude toward the Law of Moses.

For all this, Matthew drew upon a second major source, largely sayings of Jesus, whose particular format as it reached Matthew (and Luke, who also used it) is still under debate. This source, unknown to us except in the way Matthew and Luke have preserved it (and possibly in scattered sayings elsewhere) is called "Q" from the initial letter of the German word for "source," "Quelle." Q material appears extensively in these two Gospels, for instance in Matthew's Sermon on the Mount and its parallel in Luke. Note in the following excerpts both the similarities (which make us conclude to a common source) and the differences (which have led to debate over Q's composition).

Matthew 5:38-48

38 You have heard the commandment, 'An eye for an eye, a tooth for a tooth.'

39 But what I say to you is: offer no resistance to injury. When a person strikes you on the right cheek, turn and offer him the other.

40 If anyone wants to go to law over your shirt, hand him your coat as well.

41 Should anyone press you into service for one mile, go with him two miles.

42 Give to the man who begs from you. Do not turn your back on the borrower.

43 You have heard the commandment, 'You shall love your countryman but hate your enemy.'

44 My command to you is: love your enemies, pray for your persecutors.

Luke 6:27-36

27 To you who hear me, I say: Love your enemies, do good to those who hate you;

28 bless those who curse you and pray for those who maltreat you.

29 When someone slaps you on one cheek, turn and give him the other; when someone takes your coat, let him have your shirt as well.

30 Give to all who beg from you. When a man takes what is yours, do not demand it back.

31 Do to others what you would have them do to you.

45

45 This will prove that you are sons of your heavenly Father, for his sun rises on the bad and the good, he rains on the just and the unjust.

46 If you love those who love you, what merit is there in that? Do not tax collectors do as much?

47 And if you greet your brothers only, what is so praiseworthy about that? Do not pagans do as much?

32 If you love those who love you, what credit is that to you? Even sinners love those who love them.

33 If you do good to those who do good to you, how can you claim any credit? Sinners do as much.

34 If you lend to those from whom you expect repayment, what merit is there in it for you? Even sinners lend to sinners, expecting to be repaid in full.

35 Love your enemy and do good; lend without expecting repayment. Then will your recompense be great. You will rightly be called sons of the Most High, since he himself is good to the ungrateful and the wicked.

48 In a word, you must be made perfect as your heavenly Father is perfect.

36 Be compassionate, as your Father is compassionate.

Matthew 7:3-5

3 Why look at the speck in your brother's eye when you miss the plank in your own?

4 How can you say to your brother, 'Let me take that

Luke 6:41-42

41 Why look at the speck in your brother's eye when you miss the plank in your own?

42 How can you say to your brother, 'Brother, let me

speck out of your eye,' while all the time the plank remains in your own?

5 You hypocrite! Remove the plank from your own eye first; then you will see clearly to take the speck from your brother's eye.

remove the speck from your eye,' yet fail yourself to see the plank lodged in your own? Hypocrite, remove the plank from your own eye first; then you will see clearly enough to remove the speck from your brother's eye.

Other material appears only in Matthew. This he apparently gathered here and there, from oral reports, from collections of Old Testament citations, or even from his own composition. Much of this material is anti-Pharisaic in tone, reflecting how Matthew's community, and Christianity generally, struggled with Pharisaism for the soul of the Jewish people after the collapse of the Jewish revolt (66-74 AD).

To get all the extra material he wanted into his expanded Gospel and because papyrus rolls were expensive and limited in length, Matthew resorted to compressing parts of Mark, at the same time editing him and even correcting Mark's Greek as he used him. Note how Matthew in shortening Mark has heightened the miraculous element in the raising of Jairus' daughter. In Mark, the girl is on the point of dying. In Matthew, she is already dead when her father asks for Jesus' help.

Matthew 9:18-26

Mark 5:21-43

21 Now when Jesus had crossed back to the other side again in the boat, a large crowd gathered around him and he stayed close to the lake.

18 Before Jesus had finished speaking to them, a synagogue leader came up, did him reverence, and said: "My daughter has just died. Please come and lay your hand on her and she will come back to life.

19 Jesus stood up and followed him, and his disciples did the same.

20 As they were going, a woman who had suffered from hemorrhages for twelve years came up behind him and touched the tassel on his cloak.

21 "If only I can touch his cloak," she thought, "I shall get well."

22 One of the officials of the synagogue, a man named Jairus, came near. Seeing

23 Jesus, he fell at his feet and made this earnest appeal: "My little daughter is critically ill. Please come and lay your hands on her so that she may get well and live."

24 The two went off together and a large crowd followed, pushing against Jesus.

25 There was a woman in the area who had been afflicted with a hemorrhage for a dozen years.

26 She had received treatment at the hands of doctors of every sort and exhausted her savings in the process, yet she got no relief; on the contrary, she only grew worse.

27 She had heard about Jesus and came up behind him in the crowd and put her hand to his cloak.

28 "If I just touch his clothing," she thought, "I shall get well."

29 Immediately her flow of blood dried up and the feeling that she was cured of her affliction ran through her whole body.

30 Jesus was conscious at once that healing power had gone out from him. Wheeling about in the crowd, he began to ask,

"Who touched my clothing?"

31 His disciples said to him, "You can see how this crowd hems you in, yet you ask, 'Who touched me?' "

32 Despite this, he kept looking around to see the woman who had done it.

33 Fearful and beginning to tremble now as she realized what had happened, the woman came and fell in front of him and told him the whole truth.

22 Jesus turned around and saw her and said, "Courage, daughter! Your faith has restored you to health." That very moment the woman got well.

34 He said to her, "Daughter, it is your faith that has cured you. Go in peace and be free of this illness."

35 He had not finished speaking when people from the official's house arrived saying, "Your daughter is dead. Why bother the Teacher further?"

36 Jesus disregarded the report that had been brought and said to the official: "Fear is useless. What is needed is trust."

37 He would not permit anyone to follow him except Peter, James, and James' brother John.

23 When Jesus arrived at the synagogue leader's house and saw the flute players and the crowd who were making a din, he said,

38 As they approached the house of the synagogue leader, Jesus was struck by the noise of people wailing and crying loudly on all sides.

24 "Leave, all of you! The little girl is not dead. She is asleep." At this they began to ridicule him.

25 When the crowd had been put out he entered and took her by the hand, and the little girl got up.

39 He entered and said to them: "Why do you make this din with your wailing? The child is not dead. She is asleep."

40 At this they began to ridicule him. Then he put them all out. Jesus took the child's father and mother and his own companions and entered the room where the child lay.

41 Taking her hand he said to her, "*Talitha, koum,*" which means "Little girl, get up."

42 The girl, a child of twelve, stood up immediately and began to walk around. At this the family's astonishment knew no bounds.

43 He enjoined them strictly not to let anyone know about it, and told them to give her something to eat.

26 News of this circulated throughout the district.

Matthew is ever the teacher. Sometimes he rearranges Mark's material to present it more systematically, as when he transposes the parables in Mark 4:1-34 to put them with others (in Mt 13). Sometimes he reverses a more natural sequence of events to teach a point. Where Mark has Jesus calm the storm and then chide the disciples for their lack of faith once the danger is past (Mk 4:39-40), Matthew has Jesus exhort them to faith in the middle of the raging seas. Then, when his point is made, Jesus calms the storm. The instruction comes first (Mt 8:26). Where Mark has the man with the withered hand left standing in the synagogue while Jesus debates the Pharisees over the legality of curing on the Sabbath (Mk 3:1-5), Matthew clears up the legal point first, before Jesus even addresses the man (Mt 12:9-13).

Matthew continues this practice of compressing and rearranging when he includes material from Q, the source he shares with Luke. Because of this, Matthew omits the circumstance under which Jesus gives the "Our Father" in answer to his disciples' request (compare Lk 11:1-4 with Mt 6:9-13). And when the centurion seeks the cure of his servant he comes directly to Jesus in Matthew 8:5. The intermediaries of Luke 7:3-6 have been edited out of the story by Matthew.

So much for what Matthew left out. But how did he organize what he put in? Here, we are fortunate to have a key in Matthew's use of the phrase, "Now it happened when Jesus had finished . . ." This formula recurs five times, in Matthew 7:28; 11:1; 13:53; 19:1; and 26:1. Every time, it ends an extended discourse or "sermon" of Jesus. In effect, this formula divides the ministry of Jesus into five parts, each of which presents a logical stage in Jesus' earthly career.

Matthew precedes the public ministry of Jesus with two chapters theologizing about his infancy. Then Matthew follows Mark in telling of John the Baptist, the baptism of Jesus, his temptations in the desert (Matthew enlarges upon these, as does Luke), and the call of the first disciples. These preliminaries over, the "Sermon on the Mount" sets forth Jesus' program for the Christians' better righteousness (Mt 5—7). Since Jesus not only taught but acted to bring God's kingdom, Matthew relates a series of Jesus' miracles in chapters 8—9. The next "sermon" contains Jesus' instructions to his disciples who are to carry on his mission (Mt 10). Jesus and

his disciples achieve mixed results, however, and opposi-
tions as well as adherents emerge in chapters 11—12.
The next "sermon," particularly in the agricultural parables taken over from Mark, then illustrates the way the
Kingdom of God is received, sometimes fruitfully, sometimes not (Mt 13). Those who do become Jesus' disciples
confess him to be the Christ (Mt 16:13-20 finally reaches
Mark's pivotal point) and since they enter into a community of believers, Jesus' next "sermon" treats of their
relationships to one another (Mt 18). As Jesus draws
near to his death, a final "sermon" warns his disciples,
preparing them for what lies ahead and exhorting them
to continual vigilance (Mt 24—25). Matthew's Gospel
ends with the traditional narratives of the passion and
resurrection of Jesus Christ.

   With all this in mind, we may outline the Gospel of
Matthew in the following way:

Inf:	The Infancy Narratives	1—2
I:	The Platform of the Kingdom of Heaven	3—7
	(a) Preliminaries to Jesus' ministry	3—4
	(b) The sermon on the mount	5—7
II:	Bringing the Kingdom of Heaven	8—10
	(a) Jesus brings the kingdom by his miracles	8—9
	(b) The apostolic sermon	10
III:	The Varied Reception of the Kingdom of Heaven	11—13:52
	(a) The opposition grows	11—12
	(b) The parabolic sermon	13:1-52
IV:	Community Life in the Kingdom of Heaven	13:53—8
	(a) The formation of disciples	13:53—17

Within this basic framework, and particularly in his five "sermons," Matthew keeps a twofold perspective: (1) he traces the development of Jesus' ministry, and (2) he makes Jesus speak to the needs of Matthew's community.

(1) In the sermon on the mount, for instance, Jesus teaches a righteousness which is to be better than that of the scribes and Pharisees (Mt 5:20), and he teaches this with authority (Mt 7:29). His own earthly ministry being limited to the lost sheep of the house of Israel (Mt 15:24), Jesus initially confines his disciples to that mission also, as we see in the apostolic sermon (Mt 10:5-6). His opponents accuse him of collusion with the devil (Mt 12:24) and whole towns turn away from Jesus, rejecting his pleas for reform (Mt 11:20-24). But the humble accept him (Mt 12:25-30). The parable of the sower shows this diverse reception of Jesus' word and work (Mt 13:4-23). Jesus forms his disciples, warning them against false teaching, urging them to service of each other, and preparing them for his impending suffering. The lessons of the "sermon" in Matthew 18 reinforce this teaching. Compare Matthew 18:1-4 with Mark 9:33-37. Finally, as Jesus approaches his end, the struggle with his opposition becomes more intense and open (Mt 23). Jesus speaks of impending judgment (Mt 24—25).

(2) As he writes, Matthew has his own community in

mind. And sometimes he has Jesus address them directly. The sermon on the mount is given not only to the crowds but to disciples (Mt 5:1). The latter are told that not everyone who says, "Lord, Lord," will be saved, but only he who acts properly (Mt 7:21). Again, Jesus sends his Twelve only to the house of Israel in Matthew 10:5-6; yet in his instructions, Jesus speaks past them to later Christian missionaries who will be called upon to witness before rulers, kings, and even Gentiles (Mt 10:16-20). When instructing his disciples on their mutual relationships in chapter 18, Jesus speaks of referring problems to the church (Mt 18:17). And those who hear the parable of the wedding banquet learn that being in the Kingdom, in this case the church, is not enough. One has to keep clean garments to stay there; otherwise, in the visitation of the King, one might be ejected (Mt 22:11-13).

What Jesus says in Matthew, then, is not mere reminiscing on the part of the evangelist but part and parcel of the Gospel mediated to Matthew's community.

Matthew's Gospel stresses fulfillment. In Jesus and his work, God has fulfilled his promises to Israel. Over and over again, Matthew makes this point clear. Here are some sample texts:

Matthew 1:20-23: ". . . Joseph, son of David, have no fear about taking Mary as your wife. It is by the Holy Spirit that she has conceived this child. She is to have a son and you are to name him Jesus because he will save his people from their sins." All this happened to fulfill what the Lord had said through the prophet: "The virgin shall be with child and give birth to a son, and they shall call him Emmanuel," a name which means "God is with us."

Matthew 5:17: Do not think that I have come to abolish the law and the prophets. I have come, not to abolish them, but to fulfill them.

Matthew 8:16-17: As evening drew on, they brought him many who were possessed. He expelled the spirits by a simple command and cured all who were afflicted, thereby fulfilling what had been said through Isaiah the prophet: "It was our infirmities he bore, our sufferings he endured."

You may find other examples of Matthew's appeal to the scriptures and God's word in Matthew 2:5-6, 15, 17-18, 23; 3:3; 4:14-16; 11:10; 12:17-21; 13:14-15, 35; 21:4-5; 26:31, 56; 27:9. In addition, there are many allusions to the scriptures in what Matthew includes.

For Matthew, Jesus is the son of Abraham (Mt 1:1) and even more so the son of David (Mt 1:1; 12:23; 21:9, 15-16; 22:42-46) who is thus preeminently the messianic King (Mt 2:2; 21:5, 27:11, 29, 37, 42), the Son of God (Mt 3:17; 4:6; 11:27; 14:33; 16:16-17; 17:5, 24-27; 27:54) and Son of Man (Mt 10:23), who will come in the glory of his Father (Mt 16:27; 24:30) as judge of the world (Mt 19:28; 25:31) and to whom all authority in heaven and on earth has been given (Mt 28:18). In saying much of this, Matthew repeats Mark, but willingly and with his own emphasis. Jesus is the expected Messiah of Israel who has now come and is now fully constituted as Lord of all. To him, then, all Israel must submit.

If Jesus is the promised Messiah, those associated with him constitute the true Israel. They are to practice the Mosaic Law along the lines laid down by the scribes and the Pharisees where their teaching continues the

genuine traditions of Moses (Mt 23:2-3), but the disciples
are not to follow Pharisaic example. They are to practice
a better righteousness (Mt 5:20). They are to be poor in
spirit (Mt 5:3), to give good example (Mt 5:16), to engage
unostentatiously in the classic acts of Jewish piety—
almsgiving, prayer, and fasting (Mt 6:1-18), to cultivate
humility (Mt 18:3-4), mercy and forgiveness (Mt 18:21-
35), and to obey Christ's commands (Mt 7:24-27).

Jesus ran into heavy opposition during his earthly
career. His enemies—Matthew says the Pharisees—attributed his exorcisms to the devil (Mt 9:34; 12:24). They
found fault with his keeping of the Law, because he ate
with tax-collectors and sinners and so ran the risk of
ritual defilement (Mt 9:9-13), because he permitted his
hungry disciples to pluck grain on the Sabbath (Mt 12:1-
2), and because his disciples ate with unwashed hands in
defiance of "the tradition of the elders" (Mt 15:1-2).
Jesus characterizes these opponents as blind guides (Mt
23:16) and even warns his disciples against their teaching (Mt 16:6, 11-12; see Mt 23:16-21), although in general
he seems to favor their interpretation, if not their practice, of Moses (Mt 23:2-3).

Matthew carries the polemic further. In his experience, the Jews as a whole are in danger of rejecting
Jesus and his teaching, increasingly preferring the way
of the Pharisees, while Gentiles have accepted Jesus as
Messiah and have entered his church. Matthew follows
Mark in recalling Jesus' prediction of Gentile entry into
the promised kingdom.

Matthew: 8:11-12: Mark what I say! Many will
come from the east and the west and will find a
place at the banquet in the kingdom of God with
Abraham, Isaac, and Jacob, while the natural
heirs of the kingdom will be driven out into the

dark. Wailing will be heard there, and the grinding of teeth.

Matthew reinforces this prediction by inserting another after Mark's citation of scripture at the end of Jesus' parable of the wicked tenant-farmers (who represent the chosen people):

> *Matthew 21:42-43:* Jesus said to them, "Did you never read in the Scriptures, 'The stone which the builders rejected has become the keystone of the structure. It was the Lord who did this and we find it marvelous to behold'? For this reason, I tell you, the kingdom of God will be taken away from you and given to a nation that will yield a rich harvest.

But the severest judgement of Matthew on his people is found in the trial scene before Pilate:

> *Matthew 27:20-26:* Meanwhile, the chief priests and elders convinced the crowds that they should ask for Barabbas and have Jesus put to death. So when the procurator asked them, "Which one do you wish me to release for you?" they said, "Barabbas." Pilate said to them, "Then what am I to do with Jesus, the so-called Messiah?" "Crucify him!" they all cried. He said, "Why, what crime has he committed?" But they only shouted the louder, "Crucify him!" Pilate finally realized that he was making no impression and that a riot was breaking out instead. He called for water and washed his hands in front of the crowd, declaring as he did so, "I am innocent of the blood of this just man.

The responsibility is yours." The whole people said in reply, "Let his blood be on us and on our children." At that he released Barabbas to them. Jesus, however, he first had scourged; then he handed him over to be crucified.

There is no legitimate basis for anti-Semitism here. Rather, since Matthew's community is largely Jewish and thinks of itself as the true Israel, inheritors of the promises, he is deploring the calamities that have fallen recently on his own people, and he explores their cause. Because Jewish leaders have condemned Jesus and have persuaded others to reject him (Mt 27:1, 20), Matthew sees the misfortunes flowing from the Jewish revolt of 66-74 AD—loss of Jerusalem (see Mt 22:7), destruction of its Temple, crucifixion and dispersal into slavery of its people—as punishment on his own people. This catastrophe has come upon all Israel, and the true Israelites can only be saddened by it while taking its lesson to heart. Matthew interprets the history of his people from within it.

This renewed Israel which the Christians now are includes Gentiles. Evidence of this fact lies scattered throughout Matthew's Gospel. The pagan centurion's faith is praised (Mt 8:10) and the advent of many Gentiles into the Kingdom is predicted (Mt 8:11). In the name of the Servant, Jesus, the Gentiles will find hope (Mt 12:21). The Gospel will be preached throughout the world as a witness to all the nations (Mt 24:14). All nations, without distinction, are subject to judgment, and the just among them will receive their reward (Mt 25:31-46).

Perhaps the clearest indication that Matthew's church is open to all occurs in the closing of his Gospel:

The Gospel of Matthew

Matthew 28:16-20: The eleven disciples made their way to Galilee to the mountain to which Jesus had summoned them. At the sight of him, those who had entertained doubts fell down in homage. Jesus came forward and addressed them in these words: "Full authority has been given to me both in heaven and on earth; go, therefore, and make disciples of all the nations. Baptize them in the name 'of the Father, and of the Son, and of the Holy Spirit.' Teach them to carry out everything I have commanded you. And know that I am with you always, until the end of the world!"

Here is a community obviously inclusive of Jews and Gentiles which acknowledges Jesus as the expected Messiah of Israel now fully constituted with God's authority. Heir to the promises, this renewed Israel, faithful to its covenant and Law, struggles against Pharisaism for the allegiance of the old Israel while it awaits the return of its risen Lord.

In the accompanying chart, what Matthew has derived from his predecessors has been noted in sections I, II, and III A, and for further elaboration of these, see the earlier charts. In III B, some of what Matthew owes to Mark appears above the line, while the structure that Matthew imposes on all this earlier material is noted below the line.

Stages in the Growth of the Gospels (3)

I. *The Ministry of Jesus.*

II. *The Interpretation of Jesus' Ministry in the Early Church.*
   A. Apostolic Testimony and Preaching
   B. Further Teaching Answering the Needs of a Growing Community
   C. Early Attempts at Gospel Writing and Similar Materials Such as Q(uelle) = Source.

III. *The Evangelists.*
   A. Mark:

Baptist	Galilee						Judea			Jerusalem	Passion-Resurrection
1:1-8	1:14—	2:1-3:6	4:1-34	8:27-30	8:31	9:30-32	10:1	10:32-34		11:1	14—15 16
		Strife Stories	Parables	Peter's Confession	I Passion	II Predictions		III			

B. Matthew:

	Baptist	Galilee		Peter's Confession	Jerusalem 16:21	Passion Predictions I *	II	III		Passion-Resurrection
	3:1-12 4:12*	5—7	10	16:13-20	16:21	17:22-23	20:17-19		24—25	26—27 28
1—2		SM	AS	13		18			ES	
Inf				PS		CS				

Inf = Infancy Narratives
SM = Sermon on the Mount
AS = Apostolic Sermon
PS = Parabolic Sermon
CS = Church or Ecclesiastical Sermon
ES = Finalities or Eschatological Sermon

Formulas: *"From that time on, Jesus began . . ."
Mt 4:17; 16:21 (see 26:16)
"Now it happened when Jesus had finished . . ."
Mt 7:28; 11:1; 13:53; 19:1; 26:1.

Good News for *Everybody*!
The Gospel of Luke

Mark wrote our first Gospel. Matthew expanded upon it. Luke carried the process further. Tradition accords him two books, a Gospel and the Acts of the Apostles. A companion of Paul, Apostle to the Gentiles, Luke is mentioned three times in the New Testament. (1) He is included among those who are sending greetings to the Christians at Colossae in Paul's letter to that church. As Paul closes this letter, he first sends greetings from Aristarchus, Mark, and Jesus Justus, all described as men "of the circumcision" (Col 4:10-11). Then Paul mentions Epaphras, Luke, and Demas, who also send their greetings (Col 4:12-14). From this apparent distinction between the two groups, scholars have concluded that Luke was a Gentile converted to Christianity. In the same passage, Paul refers to Luke as a "beloved physician." (2) Paul once again includes Luke among those sending greetings, this time to Philemon (Phlm 24). (3) In 2 Timothy 4:11, Luke is said to be the only one with Paul in his captivity. Many authors doubt Paul wrote this last letter, but no matter. It at least testifies to the traditional linking of Luke with Paul in the apostolate.

Luke is not mentioned in either of his works, but when Paul goes about on his missionary journeys in

Acts, Luke is sometimes with him, as Luke's use of "we" in Acts 16:10-17; 20:5—21:18; 27:1—28:16 clearly shows. The close association between Paul and Luke in this early, critical period inevitably had its profound impact on Luke and appears in his theology when he finally began to write.

Just where and when Luke wrote his Gospel, however, is still unclear, although many interpreters now favor a date between 70 and 85 A.D., while continuing the traditional assignment of the Gospel to Achaia (southern Greece).

Luke does tell us why he wrote:

Luke 1:1-4: Many have undertaken to compile a narrative of the events which have been fulfilled in our midst, precisely as those events were transmitted to us by the original eyewitnesses and ministers of the word. I too have carefully traced the whole sequence of events from the beginning, and have decided to set it in writing for you, Theophilus, so that Your Excellency may see how reliable the instruction was that you received.

Luke writes, then, to reassure Theophilus. But of what? That he has been reliably instructed in the faith. Luke seems intent on counteracting any real or possible danger to Theophilus' practice of Christianity. It is not possible now to know with certainty just what trouble Theophilus might have encountered, but perhaps elements in the church continued to insist on a Christianity hostile to Gentile converts. If so, Luke points out with Pauline emphasis that salvation is offered to all equally, to Jew first it is true, but then also to the Gentiles.

To make his point that Christianity is for all, Luke

writes two books, really one work in two parts. His first book speaks of "all that Jesus did and taught until the day he was taken up to heaven" (Acts 1:1-2). In the second, Luke traces the spread of God's word from Jerusalem to Rome, from Jew to Gentile. Since this second part of his work, the Acts of the Apostles, has no precedent, Luke has greater freedom in his composition of it, and it is somewhat easier to see his development and special concerns there. But these concerns also appear in his Gospel and determine the way he treats his principal source materials, Mark and Q.

In taking over Mark, Luke, like Matthew, has happily assumed a tradition deriving from apostolic witness. The basic outline of Jesus' ministry with its culmination in Christ's resurrection forms the framework of Luke's Gospel as it did of the other two Gospels. The smaller collections of unities—strife stories, linked parables, grouped miracles—which predated Mark and were utilized by him appear again in Luke. Mark's own special structure, with its Petrine confession of Christ and its alternation of Passion prediction and apostolic failing, also finds room in Luke. In short, Luke continues the process of Gospel growth out of an earlier oral tradition based ultimately on apostolic preaching.

But Luke had something he wanted to say himself. The Gospel of Jesus was for all, and Luke lets us know of this universal offer of salvation by the way he sets about using Mark, Q, and whatever special materials are available to him. Mark's Gospel provides the basic framework into which Luke inserts blocks of material deriving from Q (a source used also by Matthew) and his special sources. Luke makes adjustments in Mark's order, adds or omits here and there, but generally reproduces the earlier Gospel as follows:

The Gospel of Luke

Mark		Luke	
1:2—3:19	=	3:1—6:19	
		6:20—8:3	Luke adds
3:31—6:44	=	8:4—9:17	
(6:45—8:26)			Luke omits
8:27—9:40	=	9:18—9:50	
		9:51—18:14	Luke adds
10:13—16:8	=	18:15—24:11	

By weaving his material together in this way and by making adjustments in it, Luke moves Jesus along his path to his death and glorification. Take your Bible now and follow this development by comparing Luke with his source Mark.

After two chapters theologizing on the births of John the Baptist and Jesus, precursor and Messiah (see Mal 3:1), Luke begins the traditional outline of Jesus' ministry with a report on the Baptist in the desert. Very tidily, Luke switches the focus from John by having Herod imprison the Baptist (Lk 3:19-20). (This allows Luke to drop the account of John's death when he reads it later, in Mark 6:17-29.) Jesus now occupies center stage. Luke continues with the usual report on Jesus' baptism by John (adding a genealogy going back to Adam, the universal father), the temptations in the desert (which Luke, like Matthew, expands), and the opening of Jesus' ministry in Galilee (the second major point in the traditional outline). Here Luke places the rejection of Jesus by his own townspeople at Nazareth (Lk 4:16-30); Mark has it later (Mk 6:1-6). This allows Luke to move Jesus to his new center of operations at Capernaum (where Mark centers the Galilean ministry). Luke follows Mark a bit, then inserts an expanded version of the call of the first disciples (Lk 5:1-11) which he had passed over earlier in Mark 1:16-20. (By omitting the call earlier, Luke had laid no foundation, as Mark had, for the mention of Simon in Luke 4:38. Jesus heals a disciple's mother-in-law before he has disciples!) From now on, Jesus is not alone. Luke continues to follow Mark to the end of the strife stories (Mk 3:6=Lk 6:11). Luke then has Jesus pick the Twelve (Lk 6:12-16), sets the scene for Jesus' preaching (Lk 6:17-19), and has Jesus deliver the "sermon on the plain" (the Lukan parallel to Matthew's sermon on the mount, Mt 5—7) (Lk 6:20-49). Mark had mentioned the preaching before the choice of the Twelve (Mk 3:7-12, 13-19).

Notice how with the Sermon Luke has moved away from Mark to follow Q and his own special materials. He continues this down to Luke 8:3. He rejoins Mark (at Mk 4) and continues with Mark to follow Jesus in his Galilean ministry as Jesus teaches and works miracles. A new stage is reached when Jesus commissions the Twelve to preach to Israel. Luke is still following Mark here, and so we can see echoes of Mark's concern (taken over by Luke) over the identity of Jesus. Herod asks: Who is he?

After the miracle of the loaves (Lk 9:12-17 = Mk 6:34-44), Luke skips over Mark 6:45—8:26 to come immediately to Peter's confession of Christ. This omission of so much Markan material by Luke puzzles scholars, but perhaps Luke wanted an immediate answer to Herod's question. Peter now reveals Jesus as the Christ or Messiah, and a new stage of Luke's development (Mark's pivotal point!) is reached (Lk 9:18-22). Luke follows Mark again past two passion predictions and apostolic failures. This brings him to Mark 9:40 = Lk 9:50, where Jesus assures his disciples that whoever is not against them is for them.

Here, at Luke 9:51, Luke breaks with Mark again

and inserts Q and special materials once more. But as he does so, Luke introduces a new emphasis in the traditional outline of Jesus' ministry. Where apostolic preaching and the other Gospels we have studied move Jesus from Galilee to Judea and Jerusalem in a rather simple fashion (Acts 10:37-40; Mk 10:1; Mt 19:1), Luke makes of this transition a solemn procession. Time and time again in this special section, Luke alludes to Jesus' journey to Jerusalem, for it is there that the prophet must die.

> *Luke 9:51:* As the time approached when he was to be taken from this world, he firmly resolved to proceed toward Jerusalem, and sent messengers on ahead of him.

> *Luke 13:22:* He went through cities and towns teaching—all the while making his way toward Jerusalem.

> *Luke 13:33:* For all that, I must proceed on course today, tomorrow, and the day after, since no prophet can be allowed to die anywhere except in Jerusalem.

> *Luke 17:11:* On his journey to Jerusalem he passed along the borders of Samaria and Galilee.

Luke maintains this emphasis on Jesus' movement toward Jerusalem when he rejoins Mark at Mark 10:13, mentioning the journey with increasing frequency in Luke 18:31 (the third passion prediction); 19:11; 19:28; 19:41; and finally in 19:45, where Jesus enters the Temple and expels the traders he finds there (echoes of Malachi 3:1-5!). From this point on, Luke generally follows Mark's order of events until the Passion-Resurrection narrative is complete. Salvation is accomplished at Jerusalem!

Luke's Gospel opened with Zechariah in the Temple praying on behalf of his people for the advent of the messianic era. Luke's Gospel ends with Jesus' disciples in the Temple praying and waiting for the new manifestation of God's power. In Luke's second book, Acts, apostolic witness carries the good news all the way from Jerusalem to Rome. Jesus tells his disciples, "You will receive power when the Holy Spirit comes down on you; then you are to be my witnesses in Jerusalem, throughout Judea and Samaria, yes, even to the ends of the earth" (Acts 1:8). All through Acts, the Gospel spreads steadily, marching in stages outward from Jerusalem. First, it reaches Hebrew and Greek speaking Jews at Jerusalem (Acts 1—7), then moves on to Judea, Galilee, and Samaria (Acts 8—12). Antioch becomes the next staging area for the spread of the Gospel, which moves from Syria to Greece (Acts 13—19). In a final, extended journey, Paul moves to his captivity in Jerusalem, Caesarea, and Rome, carrying the Gospel with him to the capital of the empire (Acts 20—28). There, Luke has Paul proclaim to the leaders of Rome's Jewish community, "Now you must realize that this salvation of God has been transmitted to the Gentiles—who will heed it!" (Acts 28:28). Geographic progression from Jerusalem to Rome has become ethnic progression from Jew to Gentile.

For Luke, this progression is evidence of a divine plan foreshadowed in the scriptures (Lk 22:37; 24:25-27, 44) and now revealed to men in its fulfillment (see 1 Cor 2:6-10). So forceful is Luke in presenting this scheme of salvation that he often portrays Jesus and others as under necessity. Jesus has to be in his Father's house

(Lk 2:49), he has to announce the good news of God's reign (Lk 4:43), he must endure many sufferings (Lk 9:22; 17:25; 22:22; 24:7), for "no prophet can be allowed to die anywhere except in Jerusalem" (Lk 13:33). The apostles must obey God and preach the Gospel (Acts 5:29), even when it brings them and their disciples to suffering (Acts 9:16; 14:22). Paul has to bear witness to Jesus in Rome (Acts 19:1; 23:11; 27:24). A plan that has to work makes certain the offer of salvation.

Why is this plan sure to work? Because the power of a dynamic Holy Spirit will see to it. God's Spirit fills the Baptist (Lk 1:15, 80) and his parents (Lk 1:41, 67), also the mother of Jesus (Lk 1:35) and the holy Simeon, who prophesies concerning Jesus' work (Lk 2:25-35). The Holy Spirit fills Jesus himself as he begins his prophetic work (Lk 3:22; 4:1, 14, 18). The Holy Spirit of God comes upon the apostles, too (Acts 1:5, 8; 2:4, 33), and it is under the guidance of this dynamic Spirit that the church moves forward in fulfilling the divine plan (Acts 4:8; 8:29, 39; 9:31; 10:19; 13:2, 4; 15:28; 20:22, 28).

Luke's general emphasis on the universality of salvation is particularized in many ways in his Gospel. Repeatedly, he expands upon his sources or includes materials not found elsewhere. When he does, the beneficiaries of salvation stand clearly revealed. They are:

(1) The poor and lowly. Mary, the mother of Jesus, praises God who "has looked upon his servant in her lowliness" and who has "deposed the mighty from their thrones and raised the lowly to high places" (Lk 1:48, 52). Jesus' birth is announced to lowly shepherds (Lk 2:8-18). At the beginning of his ministry, Jesus reads from Isaiah 61:1-2; 58:6:

> The Spirit of the Lord is upon me;
>   therefore he has anointed me.

He has sent me to bring glad tidings to the poor,
  to proclaim liberty to captives,
Recovery of sight to the blind
  and release to prisoners,
To announce a year of favor from the Lord.

(Luke 4:18-19)

When he preaches, Jesus says, "Blest are you poor" (Lk 6:20; Mt 5:3 has "poor in spirit"). Jesus responds to the Baptist's deputation:

Luke 7:22: Go and report to John what you have seen and heard. The blind recover their sight, cripples walk, lepers are cured, the deaf hear, dead men are raised to life, and the poor have the good news preached to them.

In the house of a leading Pharisee, Jesus tells his host how to give a successful banquet:

Luke 14:12-14: Whenever you give a lunch or dinner, do not invite your friends or brothers or relatives or wealthy neighbors. They might invite you in return and thus repay you. No, when you have a reception, invite beggars and the crippled, the lame and the blind. You should be pleased that they cannot repay you, for you will be repaid in the resurrection of the just.

The host (God) in the parable of the great dinner fills his house with "the poor and the crippled, the blind and the lame" (Lk 14:21). Another parable tells us of the poor beggar Lazarus who gains the benefits of the here-after (Lk 16:19-31). Time after time, Luke warns against the dangers of wealth. He has Jesus hurl woes upon the rich (Lk 6:24), warn against greed (Lk 12:15), and promise insecurity despite riches (Lk 12:16-21). Luke characterizes the Pharisees as "avaricious" (Lk 16:14) and notes how wealth kept one member of the ruling class from full discipleship of Jesus (Lk 18:18-23). Luke's message is clear—money invites the temptation to self-reliance; poverty can only have recourse to God.

(2) Sinners. The Pharisees scorned sinners (Lk 7:39; 15:1-2). But Jesus' concern for sinners appears in many places. He forgives a penitent woman (Lk 7:50), urges all to repent (Lk 13:1 5), and emphasizes God's willingness to forgive sinners in the parables of the lost sheep, lost coin, and prodigal son (Lk 15). Jesus praises repentant sinners, the tax-collector of his parable (Lk 18:9-14) and the reformed tax-collector Zacchaeus (Lk 19:1-10). On the cross, Jesus still exercises his ministry of forgiveness, reassuring the sorrowful criminal beside him, "This day you will be with me in paradise" (Lk 23:43).

(3) Women. The male-dominated society of Jesus' day gave women second place. But Luke shows that they too share in Jesus' mission and reap the benefits of his saving power. In the birth narratives, Elizabeth, Mary, and Anna figure prominently (Lk 1—2). The participation of Herodias and her daughter in the Baptist's death is suppressed (Lk 3:19-20; see Mark 6:17-29). Jesus recalls how Elijah helped the widow of Zarephath (Lk 4:26), heals Simon's mother-in-law (Lk 4:38; Mk 1:29-31; Mt 8:14-15), raises the widow of Naim's son (Lk 7:11-16), and forgives the penitent woman (Lk 7:36-50). Grateful women assist his mission of mercy (Lk 8:2-3). He raises Jairus' daughter and cures the woman who touched his cloak (Lk 8:40-56; Mk 5:21-43; Mt 9:18-26). Martha and Mary show him hospitality and hang on his words (Lk 10:38-42). A sick woman is healed in a synagogue on the Sabbath (Lk 13:10-17), and a poor woman searching for

her lost coin becomes an illustration of God's mercy (Lk 15:8-10) as another illustrates God's readiness to respond to prayer (Lk 18:1-8). The widow is praised for her whole-hearted offering (Lk 21:1-4; Mk 12:41-44). The women who assisted Jesus in his ministry are present at his death (Lk 23:49; Mk 15:40-41; Mt 27:55-56), observe his burial and prepare to anoint him (Lk 23:55-56; Mk 15:47; Mt 27:61). They are the first to discover the empty tomb and carry the news back to his apostles (Lk 24:1-11; Mk 16:1-8; Mt 18:1-8). As you can see from the references, Luke includes stories favorable to women far more than the other evangelists, for Luke wants to stress the universality of salvation. No one is second-class in God's eyes; no one is excluded.

(4) Samaritans. Luke cannot bring himself to share in the traditional hostility of Jew for Samaritan. He records the rejection of Jesus by a Samaritan village as he starts his trek toward Jerusalem. But Luke also reports that Jesus wanted no reprisals against that village (Lk 9:52-55). Luke is the only evangelist to relate the parable of the Good Samaritan (Lk 10:29-33) and the only one making the tenth, grateful leper a Samaritan (Lk 17:11-19). Forgiveness characterizes Jesus' mission; salvation can reach out to these traditional enemies as well.

(5) Gentiles. Long contact with the apostle of the Gentiles has impressed upon Luke the Gospel's openness to Gentiles. Luke expresses this not only in his geographic-ethnic march of salvation history but in many concrete examples as well. Simeon sees Jesus as a "light to the Gentiles" (Lk 2:32). Luke cites Isaiah 40:1-5 when describing the Baptist and continues the citation until he reaches "all mankind shall see the salvation of God" (Lk 3:6). The ancestry of Jesus goes back to Abraham in Matthew; in Luke, it reaches to Adam, the father of all

mankind (Lk 3:23-38). Jesus reminds his townspeople that Elijah helped Gentiles (Lk 4:25-27). A pagan centurion's faith earns his servant a cure (Lk 7:1-10). The Queen of Sheba and the men of Nineveh will condemn Israel for unbelief (Lk 11:29-32). Many will come from all directions to sit at table in the kingdom of God (Lk 13:29). In short, in Jesus' name, "penance for the remission of sins is to be preached to all the nations beginning at Jerusalem" (Lk 24:47).

Thus salvation reaches across all barriers, geographic, ethnic, and social, so that Luke's Gospel re-echoes the thought of Paul:

> *1 Corinthians 12:13:* It was in one Spirit that all of us, whether Jew or Greek, slave or free, were baptized into one body. All of us have been given to drink of the one Spirit.

> *Galatians 3:28-29:* There does not exist among you Jew or Greek, slave or freeman, male or female. All are one in Christ Jesus. Furthermore, if you belong to Christ you are the descendants of Abraham, which means you inherit all that was promised.

In the following chart, Luke's sources are noted in I, II, and IIIA, for which see earlier charts and text. Luke's own work appears on two lines, one for his Gospel and one for the book of Acts. Some of what Luke obtains from Mark lies above the line for Luke's Gospel while much of what he derives from Q and special sources is noted below that line. Only the general movement of God's word has been charted for Acts.

Stages in the Growth of the Gospels (4)

I. The Ministry of Jesus.
II. The Interpretation of Jesus' Ministry in the Early Church.
III. The Evangelists.
   A. Mark:

						Judea		Jerusalem	Passion-Resurrection
Baptist	Galilee								
1:1-8	1:14—	2:1—3:6	4:1-34	8:27-30	8:31	9:30-32	10:1 10:32-34	11:1	14—15 16
		Strife Stories	Parables	Peter's Confession	Passion	Predictions			
					I	II	III		

C. Luke:

					Passion Predictions			Jerusalem	Passion-Resurrection
Baptist	Galilee			Peter's Confession					
3:1-20	4:14—	6:20—8:3 Insertion	6:20-49 Sermon on Plain	9:18-20	9:21-22	9:43-45	18:31-34	19:45	22—23 24
1—2 Inf					I	II	III	9:51—18:14 Insertion 9:51—	
					Journey to Jerusalem				

Acts:

	Salvation offered to Jews first			Then to Gentiles		Paul's Journey to Rome
Preparation	Jerusalem	Judea, Galilee, Samaria		Antioch to Greece		
1	2—7	8—12		13—19:20		19:21—28

Divinity Among Us
The Gospel of John

More is said of the apostle John in the New Testament than of Matthew, Mark or Luke, and yet John's name is not mentioned in the Gospel attributed to him. Scholars even doubt if he is the beloved disciple mentioned several times in the fourth Gospel (e.g., Jn 13:23-26). John, the son of Zebedee and Salome (Mk 1:19; Mk 15:40 with Mt 27:56), was brother to James (the Greater) and was called with him to follow Jesus (Mk 1:19-20). The two were nicknamed "sons of thunder" (Mk 3:17), though why we do not know. John complained unsuccessfully about an unauthorized exorcist (Mk 9:38), and both brothers wanted to call down fire upon an inhospitable Samaritan village, although Jesus would hear none of it (Lk 9:54-55). The brothers tried to obtain preferred places in the coming kingdom but were only promised suffering (Mk 10:35-45).

The brothers were privileged, with Peter, to witness the healing of Peter's mother-in-law (Mk 1:29), the raising of Jairus' daughter (Mk 5:37-43), and the transfiguration of Jesus (Mk 9:2-10), but they failed Jesus in the Garden of Gethsemane (Mk 14:32-42).

After Pentecost, John worked with Peter in curing the lame man and appeared before the Jewish council with Peter on the next day (Acts 3:1—4:22). Peter and John went to Samaria to confer the Spirit upon new disciples of Jesus there (Acts 8:14). Sometime later, Paul calls John a pillar of the church at Jerusalem (Gal 2:9). Traditionally, John has been identified with the beloved disciple of John 13:23; 19:26; 20:2; 21:7, 20-23, 24.

But the apostle John did not compose John's Gospel as we have it, although his ministry and authority lie behind it. There is ample evidence for saying this. Note how the Gospel ends twice:

> *John 20:30-31*: Jesus performed many other signs as well—signs not recorded here—in the presence of his disciples. But these have been recorded to help you believe that Jesus is the Messiah, the Son of God, so that through this faith you may have life in his name.

> *John 21:24-25*: It is the same disciple who is the witness to these things; it is he who wrote them down and his testimony, we know, is true. There are still many other things that Jesus did, yet if they were written about in detail, I doubt there would be room enough in the entire world to hold the books to record them.

Evidently, chapter 21 is an appendix written later by another author. Similar literary seams can be detected elsewhere in this Gospel, but let us take only one, which occurs in the Last Supper. John 14:31 and 18:1 flow together nicely when read in succession, leaving the impression that chapters 15—17 are an alternate discourse tacked on to an earlier narrative of the Last Supper:

John 14:31: ...Come, then! Let us be on our way.

John 18:1: After this discourse, Jesus went out with his disciples across the Kidron valley. There was a garden there, and he and his disciples entered it.

Disciples obviously have been at work transmitting the Gospel according to John while adding to it and giving it its final shape. The author above all responsible for this Gospel after the apostle John remains in obscurity. But like Matthew, Mark, and Luke, the Gospel of John has its roots in an apostolic tradition. Just where and when it was put together no one can say with certainty today. Tradition locates its appearance in Ephesus toward the close of the first century, and perhaps this is as close as we can come to its publication data now.

Apostolic preaching began a traditional outline of Jesus' ministry, an outline visible in each Gospel we have seen so far. Compare the italicized elements of this traditional outline with the same elements in the structure of Mark, Matthew, and Luke:

John's Gospel

I.	Prologue	1:1-18
II.	Preparation of Jesus' Ministry	1:19-51
	John the Baptist	1:19-34
	First Disciples	1:35-51
III.	The Ministry Begins	2:1—4:54
	Cana of Galilee	2:1-11
	Cana of Galilee	4:46-54
IV.	Rejection Begins	5:1—6:71
	Cure on the Sabbath	5:1-15

We have seen how Matthew and Luke drew upon Mark. Did John know any of these three? It seems not, although this question, like so many others in the study of John, is matter for scholarly dispute. There is no question, however, that John's Gospel knew and drew upon materials similar to those we find in the other Gospels. It speaks of Jesus feeding 5,000 (Jn 6:1-15; Mk 6:33-44), Jesus walking on water (Jn 6:16-21; Mk 6:45-52), Peter's confession of Jesus (Jn 6:67-69; Mk 8:27-30), the anointing of Jesus at Bethany (Jn 12:1-8; Mk 14:3-9), Jesus' entry into Jerusalem (Jn 12:12-19; Mk 11:1-10), and his cleansing of the Temple (Jn 2:13-21; Mk 11:15-18). John may report these incidents differently for his own purposes, but their presence in his Gospel indicates that he relies on a traditional transmission of the word.

As far as John's purpose, this is clear. What is in his Gospel is there "to help you believe that Jesus is the Messiah, the Son of God, so that through this faith you may have life in his name" (Jn 20:31). This is not a totally different purpose than the other Gospels profess, but John goes about achieving it in his own way. Perhaps we can best grasp how he does this if we remember that John envisions a whole sphere of reality out of sight of this world, a reality which must be revealed to be perceived. The deeper meaning in persons and things encountered here below can be seen only by believers, to whom this inner reality has been disclosed. John's credal perspective leads him to employ some highly interesting techniques in his Gospel:

(1) *Plays upon words.* Jesus assures Nicodemus one must be born *another.* This Greek word can mean "from above" or "again." Nicodemus, not a believer, takes the crasser meaning. How can a man re-enter his mother's womb to be born again? But Jesus refers to a new life given from above. The believer perceives the correct meaning. One who functions only in this world cannot (Jn 3:1-8). The woman at Jacob's well hears Jesus say he can give her "living," that is, "flowing" water. She thinks only of some stream and notes that since Jesus has no bucket, he cannot tap even Jacob's well. But he speaks of a teaching that revivifies anyone who drinks it in (Jn 4:4-14).

(2) *Irony.* What is said about Jesus has a deeper meaning than the speaker intended. The woman at the well asks, "Surely you do not pretend to be greater than our ancestor Jacob . . .?" But he is (Jn 4:12). Jesus tells his opponents he will soon go away, and they ask, "Where does he intend to go that we will not find him? Surely he is not going off to the Diaspora, among the Greeks, to teach them?" But in fact, when John's Gospel

was published, Jesus had reached the Greeks (Jn 7:32-36). A Sanhedrin in turmoil and trying to avoid a Roman takeover asks, "What are we to do?" Caiaphas replies, "Can you not see that it is better for you to have one man die for the people than to have the whole nation destroyed?" Caiaphas wants one man, Jesus, killed to protect the nations' political situation. But unwittingly, he utters Christian theology. Jesus has died on behalf of his people (Jn 11:45-54).

(3) *Misunderstanding followed by explanation.* Jesus says, "Destroy this temple and in three days I will raise it up." His enemies misunderstand him to speak of the Herodian Temple. The true explanation follows, "Actually, he was talking about the temple of his body," as his disciples came to learn later (Jn 2:18-22). Once again, the believer has a range of reality totally unknown to the uninitiated. When Lazarus dies, Jesus goes to him. "Our beloved Lazarus has fallen asleep, but I am going there to wake him." The disciples feel sleep is good for the sick man and tell Jesus so. But "Jesus had been speaking about his death." Here again, the words have deeper meaning. Jesus raises the dead to life (Jn 11:11-15).

For John, Jesus reveals the Father, who is beyond the ordinary sight of men, for "no one has ever seen God." This God, who is spirit (Jn 4:24), remains unknown until he reveals himself through his Son. Jesus makes this point in the Temple and again at the Last Supper:

John 7:28-29: At this, Jesus, who was teaching in the temple area, cried out: "So you know me, and you know my origins? The truth is, I have not come of myself. I was sent by One who has the right to send, and him you do not know. I know him because it is from him I come; he sent me.

John 14:8-9: "Lord," Philip said to him, "show us the Father, and that will be enough for us." "Philip," Jesus replied, "after I have been with you all this time, you still do not know me? Whoever has seen me has seen the Father."

But why did God choose to reveal himself? John has the answer to that too:

John 3:16-17: Yes, God so loved the world that he gave his only Son, that whoever believes in him may not die but may have eternal life. God did not send the Son into the world to condemn the world, but that the world might be saved through him.

Jesus, then, is the apostle of his Father:

John 12:49-50: For I have not spoken on my own; no, the Father who sent me has commanded me what to say and how to speak. Since I know that his commandment means eternal life, whatever I say is spoken just as he instructed me.

It is interesting to note that John, which gives the clearest teaching on the divinity of Christ, is also the Gospel which lays most stress on Jesus' subjection to his Father in his humanity. Jesus does nothing by himself (Jn 5:19) but carries out his Father's will (Jn 4:34; 6:38). As apostle of his Father, Jesus bears witness to him (Jn 3:11, 31-32).

But Jesus must be seen as a credible witness, and for that he needs others to testify on *his* behalf. John provides a host of witnesses. The Baptist, who has come to testify to the light (Jn 1:7), points to Jesus as the Lamb of God (Jn 1:29), God's chosen one (Jn 1:34), and turns his disciples toward Jesus. (Jesus acknowledges the Baptist's testimony in Jn 5:33.) In the process of becoming Jesus' disciples, first Andrew, then Philip testifies to Jesus. Andrew calls him Messiah (Jn 1:41); Philip cites the evidence of the Law and the prophets (Jn 1:45). Nathanael, too, bears witness, "Rabbi, you are the Son of God; you are the king of Israel" (Jn 1:49). Later on, Peter reaffirms this faith (Jn 6:68-69).

Other witness shows up. Jesus says, "The works I do in my Father's name give witness in my favor" (Jn 10:25). Nicodemus admits this, "Rabbi, we know you are a teacher come from God, for no man can perform signs and wonders such as you perform unless God is with him" (Jn 3:2). God, then, is chief witness for Jesus, as he asserts, "The Father who sent me has himself given testimony on my behalf" (Jn 5:37; see 8:18). The Father has even planted evidence in the Scriptures pointing to Jesus, who tells unbelievers, "Search the Scriptures in which you think you have eternal life—they also testify on my behalf" (Jn 5:39). Ironically, unbelievers add their evidence. The woman at the well (Jn 4:12), the Jews (Jn 7:35), and Caiaphas (Jn 11:49-52) all testify to Jesus.

All this testimony demands a verdict. The signs, the witness in this Gospel, have been recorded "to help you believe" (Jn 20:31). There is here a challenge, a demand. One cannot ignore it, for as Jesus puts it when replying to questioners, "This is the work of God; have faith in the one whom he sent (Jn 6:29). Whoever rejects Jesus "already has his judge" and the word Jesus has spoken will condemn him on the last day (Jn 3:18; 12:48). For unbelievers dwell in darkness (Jn 3:20; 12:35, 46) and death (Jn 5:24). But the believer who accepts Jesus becomes a child of God (Jn 1:12). Jesus tells such believers,

"If you live according to my teaching you are truly my disciples; then you will know the truth, and the truth will set you free" (Jn 8:31-32). Believers have light, a symbol of happiness and of God's presence (Jn 8:12); they have life, which all men desire (Jn 5:21; 6:56-57; 8:12; 10:28); and they know by experience the truthful God (Jn 3:33; 8:32).

Jesus, John tells us, came to his own, who did not receive him (Jn 1:11). "Despite many signs performed in their presence, they refused to believe in him" (Jn 12:37). About one half of John's Gospel, the "Book of Signs," is taken up by these rejected evidences (Jn 1— 12). In the remainder, the "Book of Glory," Jesus becomes manifest as king of Israel (Jn 13—21). He does so by laying down his life in obedience to the Father's command:

> *John 10:17-18:* The Father loves me for this: that I lay down my life to take it up again. No one takes it from me; I lay it down freely. I have the power to lay it down, and I have the power to take it up again. This command I received from my Father.

As in the other Gospels, Jesus' death is seen as fulfillment of the divine plan for salvation. But note the difference. In John, Jesus' death is a triumph. No one takes his life from him against his will. When the soldiers come to take him in the garden of Gethsemane, Jesus speaks a word, and the soldiers tumble to the ground. When Peter strikes out in his behalf, Jesus stays his hand (Jn 18:3-11). Pilate learns that not he but a higher hand is in control of Jesus' fate (Jn 19:10-11). Once Jesus has fulfilled the scripture, but only then, and according to plan, he bows his head and dies (Jn 19:28-

30). This glorious abasement is ultimate victory, for God has established Jesus as Messiah. John expresses this even during Jesus' suffering, constantly designating him as king (Jn 18:33, 37, 39: 19:3, 12, 14, 15, 19, 21).

But Jesus is more than Messiah, more than Son of God in a human sense, however exalted. It is now clear to John and those who believe that Jesus is himself God.

> In the beginning was the Word;
> the Word was in God's presence,
> and the Word was God.
>
> *John 1:1*

All through John's Gospel, Jesus' divinity overshadows his humanity. The Word of God who became flesh (Jn 1:14) speaks with an affirmation used of God in the earlier scriptures, "I Am" (Ex 3:14; Is 43:13). Note how often Jesus uses this style and the variations he plays upon it:

> *John 8:24:* You will surely die in your sins unless you come to believe that I Am.

> *John 8:28:* When you lift up the Son of Man, you will come to realize that I Am and that I do nothing by myself.

> *John 8:58-59:* Jesus answered them [the Jews]: I solemnly declare it: before Abraham came to be, I Am. At that they picked up rocks to throw at Jesus, but he hid himself and slipped out of the temple precincts.

> *John 13:19:* I tell you this now, before it takes place, so that when it takes place you may believe that I Am.

Jesus also says, "I am" the bread of life (Jn 6:35, 48, 51), the bread that came down from heaven (Jn 6:41); "I am" the light of the world (Jn 8:12); "I am" the sheepgate, through which the sheep enter to safety (Jn 10:7, 9); "I am" the good shepherd himself (Jn 10:11, 14); "I am" the resurrection and the life (Jn 11:25); "I am" the way and the truth and the life (Jn 14:6). Again, the believer knows the inner meaning of this usage. Jesus is more than mere man. With Thomas, the believer cries out, "My Lord and my God" (Jn 20:28).

Since Jesus and his Father are one (Jn 10:30) in their action on behalf of his disciples, Jesus prays for unity between Christians patterned on the same divine model:

John 17:20-23: I do not pray for them [his first disciples] alone. I pray also for those who will believe in me through their word, that all may be one as you, Father, are in me, and I in you; I pray that they may be [one] in us, that the world may believe that you sent me. I have given them the glory you gave me that they may be one, as we are one—I living in them, you living in me—that their unity may be complete. So shall the world know that you sent me, and that you loved them as you loved me.

Union with Jesus, the vine in which Christians are branches (Jn 15:1, 5), permits union with the Father through Jesus and brings about a higher, divine form of life for the Christian.

John has yet one theme to strike. Jesus had not returned. And those who heard John's Gospel in its development were anxious. What of the meantime?

What are we to do until he comes again? Like Luke, John found the answer in the Holy Spirit. In Luke's Acts, the Spirit is dynamic, moving the church outward and onward. In John, the Spirit is immanent. The Spirit of truth or Paraclete will remain with the church always (Jn 14:16) to instruct it in everything and to bring to mind all that Jesus taught (Jn 14:26). This Spirit of truth will be one more witness to Jesus, strengthening his church in its time of persecution (Jn 15:26). In short, the Spirit will perform for the disciples all those functions that Jesus did while he was with them. Jesus is the truth; the Paraclete is the Spirit of truth.

The few points made in these pages have shown that John's Gospel emphasizes traditional themes in its own way. This is an incarnational Gospel; the divine is humanized. Jesus is truly man and as Messiah goes along the path foreseen for him. But he is also God and the one who reveals God to man. Whoever believes in Jesus comes to see him for what he is and enters into a new, a higher relationship with the Father through him—and has life more abundantly.

One Final Word

We have now looked at all four Gospels, noting their sources, their structures, and their theologies. Each has proved to be a highly individualized view of Jesus and his work, yet a view expressed within a framework of commonality. In each Gospel, we can detect successive stages of growth, from Jesus' earthly ministry through the apostolic preaching and its development to the theologies of the evangelists. Consequently, we learn that the Gospels are products of the church as well as of gifted individuals. This church is traditional enough to want sound roots for its Gospel in the past, creative enough to reshape its Gospel message for new situations. The pastoral needs of the church in Rome, Syria, Greece, and Asia helped give distinctive form to what the evangelists set down centuries ago. A similar pastoral concern must, and does, motivate the church today, for it still has to proclaim this Gospel message: Christ has died, Christ is risen, Christ will come again.

A Dozen Good Books

This simple bibliography lists a dozen readable and generally reliable works which will help introduce you to further biblical study. To add more books here may be too much. When you are ready for more, the recommended works will provide additional bibliography.

Anderson, Bernhard, *Understanding the Old Testament* (3rd ed. Prentice-Hall, 1975)

Barclay, William, *The Men, the Meaning, the Message of the New Testament Books* (Westminster, 1978)

Bright, John, *A History of Israel* (2nd ed. Westminister, 1972)

Brown, Raymond E., *et al., The Jerome Biblical Commentary* (Prentice-Hall, 1968)

Bruce, Frederick F., *New Testament History* (Doubleday, 1972)

Giblin, Charles H., *In Hope of God's Glory* (Herder and Herder, 1970)

Lohse, Edward, *The New Testament Environment* (Abingdon, 1976)

McKenzie, John L., *Dictionary of the Bible* (Bruce, 1965)

May, Herbert, *Oxford Bible Atlas* (2nd ed. Oxford, 1974)

Neill, Stephen, *Jesus Through Many Eyes* (Fortress, 1976)

Perkins, Pheme, *Reading the New Testament* (Paulist, 1978)

Vermes, Geza, *The Dead Sea Scrolls: Qumran in Perspective* (Collins, 1978)